SEX
AND THE
CITY
THE MOVIE

WRITTEN & DIRECTED BY
MICHAEL PATRICK KING

INTRODUCTION BY
SARAH JESSICA PARKER

WRITTEN BY
AMY SOHN

DESIGNED BY
NUMBER SEVENTEEN

PHOTOGRAPHS BY
CRAIG BLANKENHORN

HarperCollins books may be purchased for educational,
business, or sales promotional use. For information, please write:
Special Markets Department, HarperCollins Publishers,
10 East 53rd Street, New York, NY 10022.

FIRST EDITION

Library of Congress Cataloging-in-Publication Data
is available upon request.

ISBN: 978-0-06-1686115

10 9 8 7 6 5 4 3 2 1

Photo credits, which constitute an
extension of this copyright page,
appear on page 176.

This book was produced by

MELCHER
MEDIA
www.melchermedia.com

Printed in China

contents

FROM
MICHAEL PATRICK
KING

After the most satisfying run of my professional career, I was approached to write and direct the *Sex and the City* movie. My immediate response was cautious: "Interesting . . . let me think about it." But that night, I couldn't sleep. As soon as someone even mentioned opening that door, ideas started to pour out of me. It was as if Carrie, Miranda, Charlotte, and Samantha had been there all along, waiting and ready to come back.

I felt the movie should be large in scope—an experience. And in order for the audience to experience what I wanted "the girls" to experience, I decided the movie should span a year. Well, I guess I got my wish, because when I printed out the first draft of the script, it was 365 pages long. It seemed that these women—or I—had a lot to say. So, I took my American version of *The Sisters Karamazov* and sequestered myself in a small hotel room in the California desert (with running water but no television) to see which of the scenes would emerge victorious.

Part of the reason the script was so long was that I was writing for four icons, each with loyal fans who were waiting to see how their favorite girl's life had turned out. I always knew that the Carrie wedding was the "Big" story left untold, so I built the script around that. Would they or wouldn't they? Typical romantic comedies build to seeing the girl in the gown at the end, but I thought, What if the wedding fell apart early on? Then what? I didn't want a wedding to be the defining moment in Carrie's journey—it was too easy, and not very "Carrie."

Nine bloody rounds later, I emerged with a shooting script and a sunburn. Left behind on the hotel room floor: Charlotte's braless nanny; Miranda's angry post-breakup dating montage; Samantha's other Hollywood client, an anorexic starlet named Ginny Lynn—whom the tabloids nicknamed "Thinny Thin"; and Carrie's rebound fling with a Ron Perelman type named Mr. Bigger.

Like all relationships that don't last despite the love, these scenes were gone. Now—impossible as it seemed—it was time to make the movie and direct these amazing actresses one more time. I was going from the desert to *dessert*. And in their hands my words became heartbreak and laughter, and this fictional year in their lives became real. As Carrie says, "I guess in some houses fairy tales do come true."

Michael Patrick King

FROM SARAH JESSICA PARKER

So here we are. When we wrapped the show on February 4th, 2004, at nearly three in the morning, I never imagined that four years later we would be saying good-bye to each other all over again. But first we had to say hello. As you may have heard over the last few years, this movie was alive, then dead, and then alive again. But the important thing is that in summer 2007 it was alive, and a go, and more real then ever. And we got to start the process all over again.

There was an enormous amount that had to be done in far too little time. Our writer and director, Michael Patrick King, had locked himself away for months to write what I knew would be a movie worth waiting for. As far back as spring 2006 (when it still wasn't entirely clear we would be making the movie), I recall making endless lists, all day long and in the middle of the night, of every little and big thing that simply had to be done. Things had to be retrieved—set pieces from all over the globe, and props that may or may not have existed anymore (never mind personally begging the Smithsonian to let us borrow Carrie's desk, which to our great honor had become a permanent exhibit at the museum. Thank goodness

they were lovely and so helpful, because my superstition and nostalgia might not have allowed me to shoot the movie without that desk). And we had to try to get a commitment from all the crew members I felt we couldn't make the movie without. All the people, all the sets, all the details, getting everyone and everything back together at the right time and in the right place—the odds seemed insurmountable, but the effort was worth every dead end and missed opportunity and impossible task.

This particular project, more than anything else I have worked on, takes on extraordinary meaning to me. And I think it's because of our audience. They have always inspired us, and we have pushed ourselves to be the best we can be—in part because we couldn't and wouldn't do it any other way, but also because the people who have invested so much time and affection deserve nothing less. All these years later it remains an honor, a privilege, a wonderful challenge, and a fervent wish to be everything you, our audience, want us to be. We hope we have lived up to your expectations. And we thank you all from the bottom of our hearts for giving us this opportunity, once again.

Sarah Jessica
xox

THE STORY BEGINS

Talk of a *Sex and the City* movie started even before the show had wrapped in February 2004—after ninety-four episodes, countless Emmy® Awards, and tremendous critical and popular success—but it would be nearly four full years before production began. "There was a desire to make a movie because the show had always felt like a movie," says series executive producer and movie writer-director Michael Patrick King. "I think people also wanted to see what had happened to the girls after the finale, but it wasn't clear how a movie would work."

Soon before the show ended its last season, King worked up a detailed outline for a movie that bears little resemblance to the final version. "With the exception of the Carrie-Big story," he explains, "it was totally different. The girls were exploring

**WRITER AND DIRECTOR
MICHAEL PATRICK KING**

being away from each other, whereas the final film is ultimately about their reunion."

Recalls actress Sarah Jessica Parker, "It was a road movie. It reminded me of a Bob Hope–Bing Crosby film, a romp."

As the show's popularity grew during syndication over the next few years, HBO considered revisiting the idea of a movie. "The series was as popular as ever," explains King, "and HBO was hearing that people were watching every night. They started to understand that a movie could do extremely well."

Meanwhile, Parker had not lost her enthusiasm. "Around April 2006," she explains, "I started thinking that it might be the right time for a movie. I talked to [former HBO chairman and CEO] Chris Albrecht about it, and he was interested." In the fall of 2006, talks between King, Parker, and HBO began in earnest.

FINDING THE WORDS

King got to work right away and pitched a story outline to Parker in New York on January 2, 2007. Encouraged by her positive reaction, he began writing the script. In mid-March, Parker remembers, "He turned in 'the masterpiece,' as it was called. It was essentially Season Seven of the show, a 365-page script that I still have not read."

"When I sat down to write it," King recalls, "I was thinking, I have a whole season to tell a story. That's why it was so long. I wanted it to have an epic feel—I wanted a lot to happen, and I wanted it to span a year." In the masterpiece, Charlotte had a story line with a too-sexy nanny; Carrie dated someone named Mr. Bigger, who was meant to be a Ron Perelman type; and there was much more about Samantha living in Los Angeles and being part of a couple.

Immediately, King began rewriting, paring the script down to a more manageable length. He wanted Big and Carrie to marry, but he didn't want to end with the wedding. "The happy ending of the movie is not 'Find a man to marry you.' It's 'Learn to celebrate yourself, and find friends who celebrate you.'"

Even when he was satisfied with the Big-Carrie story line, King had to find a way to include four other story lines (Miranda's, Charlotte's, Samantha's, and Carrie's assistant, Louise's) while keeping the script to a reasonable length. "The script had to be more streamlined than a typical romantic comedy," he explains, "and it had to rely more on the characters' stories and emotions, rather than their dialogue at every moment."

But King never considered cutting Louise, even for streamlining purposes. "I wanted there to be a twentysomething girl in the movie, because the story is really about twentysomething girls becoming fortysomething women." He also wanted to add someone new to the cast. "I felt that the girls had said everything they could say about Carrie and Big. I wanted someone with a new perspective."

When Parker read the revised script in the spring of 2007, she loved it. "There were things that weren't in there, but I understood why he didn't put them there. And I knew that things that could only be hinted at on the page would be gigantic on-screen."

GETTING THE GREEN LIGHT

It was crucial to Parker that production begin quickly so that the film could be released by summer 2008. "I knew it was not something we could come back to again," she says. "It was now or never. You can only work so hard to get something made so many times." Says King, "We were constantly in and out, not knowing if we had a deal or not."

In May 2007, the *Sex and the City* team was thwarted again when Chris Albrecht stepped down as chairman and CEO of HBO. Soon after, HBO decided it would not produce the movie because, according to King, it was too big for the type of movies that Picturehouse, its feature-film arm, usually makes.

"I really wanted to keep it in the Time Warner family," says Parker, "because I felt there was a sensibility that Michael and I could protect." Both New Line and Warner Bros. were interested, but in the end the film went to New Line.

Because King, Parker, and producer John Melfi were ready to hire almost the entire original creative team from the series, preproduction only took eight weeks instead of the typical twelve or sixteen. All of the key players knew each other and had already developed a working relationship.

She hurries up the street to Big's car holding her bouquet.
Big gets out of his car just as Carrie reaches him.

> BIG
> I freaked out for a minute -- but --
> I'm ready now --

Carrie HITS him with her bouquet. It's a violent direct hit
on his face. He recoils. She hits him again, hard... a
wounded sound escaping her throat.

> BIG (CONT'D)
> Carrie!

She hits him again. He ducks back into the car for
protection. She hits the bouquet on the roof of the car --
the flowers start breaking apart and flying everywhere.

> CARRIE
> I knew you would do this -- I knew
> it!

Miranda reaches Carrie and holds her back by her waist. Big   *
gets back out of the car and starts over to her.

> BIG
> I'm sorry -- I just --

With all she has left, she throws the broken bouquet at him.

> CARRIE
> You left! I am humiliated!

Carrie starts crying. Charlotte has arrived. Carrie turns and
falls into her arms. Miranda and Charlotte lead her away. Big
starts over to follow.

> BIG
> Carrie, wait --

Charlotte whips her head around and stares him down.

> CHARLOTTE
> No!

He stops in his tracks. A WAITRESS (20's) at the Brant Park   *
Cafe nearby "over-pours" water into a CUSTOMER'S glass --   *
riveted by the scene. Miranda and Charlotte move Carrie back   *
into the limo. A CAB comes down the street and HONKS at Big   *
standing in the road; dazed.

LIGHTS, CAMERA, MANHATTAN!

Production began September 19, 2007, in New York City and wrapped January 15, 2008, in Malibu, California. The movie was shot in sixty-nine days, much of it on location in New York, with a few scenes in and around Los Angeles. Key New York locations included the New York Public Library, Bryant Park, the restaurant Buddakan, Bemelmans Bar in the Carlyle Hotel, the Brooklyn Bridge, the Central Park Reservoir, Perry Street (Carrie's apartment), Tiffany & Co., and the Brooklyn Supreme Court (as a stand-in for City Hall). Challenges included coping with changing weather (some warm scenes were shot in cold weather and vice versa); coordinating three hundred costume changes for the four women; managing three children, several dogs, and even one mayor of New York City on set; and, of course, dealing with the constant interruptions of fans and paparazzi—who sometimes numbered in the hundreds.

Still, the cast and crew are universally positive about their experiences on the film, largely because of the actor-friendly work environment created by King. "The environment was so supportive, there was no way we could fail," says Kim Cattrall. "All we could do was succeed and have fun."

THE FAN FRENZY

The presence of fans created endless production obstacles on the set. On one of Parker's first days, while shooting at Tiffany & Co., filming had to be delayed because of difficulties managing the crowds. "We can only ask for two police officers, because the city has bigger problems than us," Parker explains. "And even though we had a lot of production assistants, we couldn't expect them to control five or six hundred people. We're talking about twenty-five-year-old girls who weren't really accustomed to being that aggressive."

The first day Parker, Cattrall, Kristin Davis, and Cynthia Nixon were all on set together, several hundred people gathered on the median of Park Avenue to watch the shoot. "That was a massive day," says camera operator Joe Collins. "Once they realized what we were shooting, the number of onlookers started to swell. As each girl arrived, they would start cheering and clapping and saluting, and finally when all four arrived it was like street theater. Every time we yelled, 'Cut!' there was a roar up and down Park Avenue for about five blocks. It gave us all an inkling of what we were in for."

All of the attention came as a surprise to the cast, who had never had to deal with so many spectators, even during the show's final season. But it was flattering. As King puts it, "The good aspects of having so much fan interest definitely outweighed the bad. Can you imagine doing a movie and no one caring?"

THE PAPARAZZI

The cast and crew had a harder time dealing the presence of the paparazzi, who could not be removed from the set, no matter how distracting they were, due to freedom of the press. "When we were shooting on Park Avenue," says Parker, "there were probably forty or fifty photographers gathered around the camera. It's very hard to work when during the silences all you hear is 'Click-click-click-click-click.' Even during the last season of the series, when we were observed by the press pretty regularly, the paparazzi presence wasn't nearly as intense."

The paparazzi created a shooting distraction of their own that day on Park Avenue. "They aren't allowed to be around the camera for takes, just for rehearsals," explains Collins, "so during the take they all piled onto the median, crawling over each other like lobsters in a tank. We were just about to

do a take when we heard a big commotion. It was four photographers getting into a brawl over their positioning for the shot. The police had to break it up."

Associate producer Melinda Relyea also noticed the presence of a whole new breed of paparazzi: "Young girls in miniskirts and Ugg boots and guys in their early twenties, all of whom looked like fans, would show up daily to snap pictures and make some money."

Evan Handler, who plays Harry, encountered *Sex and the City* fever during production. "I met a couple of reporters at the restaurant P.J. Clarke's who told me they wrote for Page Six of the *New York Post*. I was hiccupping, and I told them I had been hiccupping throughout the day. The next thing I knew, there was a series of articles making the rounds about what they called my 'chronic hiccupping condition' that I've had for two years. I sent the reporters e-mail messages saying, 'What are you doing?' So then the story became, '*Sex and the City* star denies that his hiccupping delayed filming.'"

Parker's biggest issue with the paparazzi presence was that it prevented the cast and crew from spending time together except when they were shooting. "When we were doing the show, I used to be able to hang out on the set with the crew, but

I couldn't do that during the movie because the paparazzi were documenting every move I made. They made it impossible for me just to sit and spend time with the crew between takes; instead, we all had to retreat to our trailers.

LOOSE LIPS SINK SCRIPTS

The biggest challenge posed by the fans and paparazzi was the danger of plot leaks. Everyone who received a script had his or her name watermarked on each individual page to prevent photocopying, and the last several pages were omitted so no one would know the ending. Parker went so far as to put a fake cover on her script (its title: *National Park* by Jesse Lasky) to throw off any prying eyes.

Because King wanted key plot points to remain secret until the film's release, he made a few last-minute changes to the shooting schedule to keep the mystery alive. For the scene between Carrie and Big on 41st Street outside the New York Public Library, he shot an alternate ending where Carrie kissed him instead of hitting him with her bouquet. Fans and even extras speculated that the entire wedding was a dream—they simply couldn't believe that any *Sex and the City* movie would end with Carrie and Big tying the knot.

When Charlotte and Big have their confrontation right before her water breaks, "someone around the camera suggested that it was a fantasy, too," says King, so some fans believed Charlotte never actually becomes pregnant. And the scene where the girls surprise Carrie after her wedding at City Hall was supposed to be shot outside Brooklyn Supreme Court—but at the last minute King moved the entire shoot indoors to keep fans surprised.

Recalls on-set still photographer Craig Blankenhorn, "It really got to Michael Patrick that so much about the movie was being discussed in the media. I thought it was amazing that he came up with the idea to shoot the wedding scene inside because he wanted it to be a surprise for everyone. He lives, eats, and breathes *Sex and the City*."

"I was very aware that everything we did would be covered in the media," says King, "but I couldn't control what happened when we were outside. I'm really happy, though, that there was nothing in the press about how the movie ends."

NO MORE WORDS

As if all of this wasn't enough to make a crew apoplectic, six weeks after production started, the Writers Guild of America went on strike, preventing King

from making any last-minute changes to the script on set. "When I knew the strike was being called for a Monday morning at midnight," he remembers, "I stayed up for three days straight the weekend before to do what I call my 'psychic rewrites.' They were psychic because I had to guess which scenes might not work when we filmed them. There is a huge difference between writing and directing—you really need to detach to write, whereas directing is very immediate. It was challenging having to direct during the day and then go home and stay up all night writing."

King ended up making some changes to the Samantha-Dante story line, changing the tone of the fashion show, and rewriting much of the Mexico sequence because he wanted to meet the expectations of what could happen to the girls in Mexico. "At midnight, I handed everything in and didn't write a thing after that."

IT'S A WRAP

Production for Parker, Nixon, and Davis ended on December 19, 2007, in a surprisingly low-key way. The last scene Parker shot was her reaction to the girls taking care of her during her Mexicoma. The crew could not secure the original location, a house,

so they used a shed in Simi Valley that smelled of gas, paint, and manure, brought in the set, and shot there until four in the morning. "There were pools of oil on the floor, and it was raining," recalls Melfi. "It was anticlimactic but funny—the most inauspicious way to end the shoot." But in spite of it all, the work done there remains some of King's favorite in the finished film. "Even though we ended in a shed," he says, "the whole filming experience was such a thrill for all of us that it didn't really matter where we finished shooting."

Parker echoes King's sentiment when she sums up the message of the film: "While that shed in Simi Valley seemed the least likely place to end this very New York–centric movie, the tone of the scene couldn't have illustrated more accurately what *Sex and the City* is about—friends taking care of each other. The four women are always there for each other, through the joy and laughter, through success and failure, but most important of all, through life's darkest, most difficult moments. That's the story our show and movie tell. And that's the story we were lucky enough to be shooting when we called the final 'Wrap' on this extraordinary adventure."

PREVIOUSLY ON
SEX AND THE CITY

CARRIE meets Mr. Big when she accidentally drops her purse, scattering condoms on the sidewalk. After meeting a sweet underwear model and dating a scruffy twentysomething, she finally sleeps with Big and the two begin an on-again, off-again affair. But Big keeps throwing Carrie curveballs that shake her romantic notions: She finds out he's been married before, and when he introduces her to his mother, she has no idea who Carrie is.

CHARLOTTE, a "Rules" girl, endures a series of romantic humiliations, agrees to pose for a painting of her vagina, gets out of her own threesome, and finally visits a fortune-teller who predicts she will never marry, horrifying her.

MIRANDA dates Carrie's friend Skipper, pretends to be a lesbian to get ahead at her law firm, later sees Skipper with another woman and jealously takes him back, and then breaks up with him while he's still inside her.

SAMANTHA fools around with a guy who talks her into being videotaped while they have sex and later faces the first of several penis-size problems when she falls for James, a guy whose dick is like a gherkin."

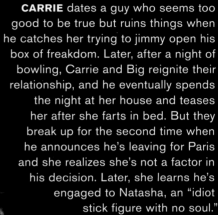

CARRIE dates a guy who seems too good to be true but ruins things when he catches her trying to jimmy open his box of freakdom. Later, after a night of bowling, Carrie and Big reignite their relationship, and he eventually spends the night at her house and teases her after she farts in bed. But they break up for the second time when he announces he's leaving for Paris and she realizes she's not a factor in his decision. Later, she learns he's engaged to Natasha, an "idiot stick figure with no soul."

CHARLOTTE tries to be adaptable, asking a guy out for the first time in her life, putting up with a crotch adjuster and a man who falls asleep while having sex with her, and suffering a bout of crabs after a Hamptons fling with a twenty-something. Finally, she decides she'd rather ride horses than put up with men.

MIRANDA begins to realize the hazards of being a successful single woman. She jilts the girls for being too man-obsessed, buys an apartment alone, and falls for a bartender named Steve—but then breaks up with him over class differences. She reunites with him after refusing to return his FDNY T-shirt, finally opening herself up to love.

Deciding that she can't ignore his "shortcomings," **SAMANTHA** breaks up with James. She plans revenge on a mean ex but then realizes she still cares about him. Later, she meets Mr. Cocky, who is more than she can handle, earning him the moniker "Goldicocks."

SEASON THREE

CARRIE meets a furniture designer named Aidan, falls for him, tries to quit smoking, and begins a secret affair with Big, who tells her he loves her. She confesses the affair to Aidan and is devastated when he won't forgive her.

CHARLOTTE declares that this is the year she will marry—and is later proven right. She meets Dr. Trey MacDougal after nearly being run over by his cab, learns to put up with his overbearing mother, discovers he can't get it up but marries him anyway, walks in on him masturbating to *Juggs* magazine, and finally suggests the two of them separate after she kisses his gardener and he seems unperturbed.

MIRANDA lets Steve move in with her, puts up with his skid marks, then breaks up with him after getting tired of being the mean mom. Later, she has a hot phone-sex fling with a new guy and makes a date with another who dies the night they're supposed to go out.

SAMANTHA dates a short man, moves to the Meatpacking District, becomes a Viagra junkie, meets a guy who insists she take an HIV test, and gets invited to the Playboy mansion on a trip with the girls to L.A.

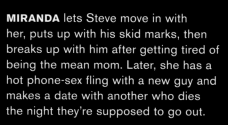

SEASON
FOUR

CARRIE spends her thirty-fifth birthday alone, but Big later surprises her with balloons and champagne. Missing Aidan, she tells him she's changed and reunites with him. He proposes to her and she accepts—but she has trouble wearing the ring and finally admits that she's not ready for marriage. When she tries to reach out to Big, she is devastated to learn that he is moving to California.

CHARLOTTE reunites with Trey after the separation proves good for his John Thomas, and she decides that it's time for them to start a family. But after much effort, she learns she has only a 15 percent chance of getting pregnant. When Trey proves unsupportive and suggests that they stop trying to have a baby, Charlotte decides to end the relationship for good.

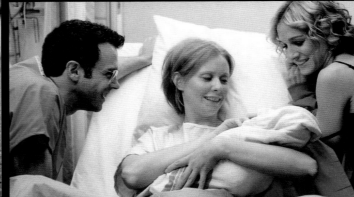

MIRANDA'S mother dies, and the girls come rushing to her side. She decides to stay friends with Steve, going so far as to have sex with him after he gets testicular cancer. Much to her surprise, she gets pregnant, decides to keeps the baby, and names him Brady Hobbes.

SAMANTHA begins a lesbian relationship with Maria but breaks things off because she can't stand all the talking. After she meets a brash hotelier named Richard Wright, the two commence a passionate affair, and she eventually tells him she's in love with him.

SEASON FIVE

CARRIE lands a book deal and meets a charismatic writer named Jack Berger, who unfortunately has a girl-friend. While on her book tour in San Francisco, she meets up with Big. She hopes for a romantic evening, but they don't end up sleeping together. And at a wedding in the Hamptons, she meets up with Berger—now newly unattached—again.

CHARLOTTE meets Harry Goldenblatt, her Jewish divorce lawyer, who admits he finds her incredibly sexy. Despite her misgivings—he's bald, sweaty, and has a hairy back—she sleeps with him, and the sex is amazing.

MIRANDA adapts to the challenges of motherhood. She tries to shed her baby weight by attending Weight Watchers, where she meets Tom, an overeater who overeats her. Later, on a date with an old flame, she gets cock-blocked by her own son.

SAMANTHA announces she's back together with Richard, but she breaks up with him when she realizes she can't trust him.

CARRIE starts dating Berger, but he breaks up with her on a Post-It note. Later, she falls in love with artist Aleksandr Petrovsky and decides to move with him to Paris, but when they get there Petrovsky is preoccupied with work and leaves her feeling abandoned. She tells him she thinks she's made a mistake, and he accidentally slaps her. Big (whose name is revealed to be John) comes to her rescue and whisks her back to New York.

CHARLOTTE converts to Judaism, but her first Shabbat ends badly when she and Harry fight. They make up and get married, but later, when they try to get pregnant, Charlotte suffers a miscarriage. After an American adoption goes awry, Harry and Charlotte receive a photo of the baby girl they plan to adopt from China.

MIRANDA realizes she still loves Steve, but he's seeing someone else. She dates Robert, a new tenant in her building, but finally reunites with Steve at Brady's first birthday party. Eventually, they get married and move to Brooklyn.

SAMANTHA begins dating an aspiring actor named Jerry Jerrod, takes him on as her client, and changes his name to Smith Jerrod. Later, she relapses with Richard but decides she cares for Smith more. When she learns she has breast cancer, she begins chemo and shaves her head—and Smith proves to be just the support she needs.

Four years and many
(monogamous)
scores later,

Charlotte

was happily married to Harry and
was raising a little girl named Lily,

Samantha

had moved to Los Angeles with Smith
but wasn't sure she liked being
so far away from her friends and New York,

Miranda

had settled down in Brooklyn
with Steve and Brady, and

Carrie

had stayed exactly where she was…
in love.

This is where our story begins.

Having settled into a comfortable relationship, Big and Carrie decided to look for an apartment together on Fifth Avenue. The hunt was proving difficult, and after the thirty-third apartment turned out to be just as awful as the rest, they started to lose hope.

"Finding the perfect apartment in New York City is like finding the perfect partner. It can take years."

CARRIE

MICHAEL PATRICK KING, WRITER AND DIRECTOR *We searched high and low for this apartment. I wanted the audience to get swept up in the fantasy of a man loving a woman enough to buy her this gorgeous home. It's a rare romantic gesture from Big—it shows his commitment to Carrie. But it's also the first trap. After the romance comes the financial reality—and Carrie's fear of one day being locked out. The penthouse is the cheese in the mousetrap of marriage.*

But all was not lost, because there was another apartment in the same building that wasn't yet on the market—the penthouse. It was perfect in every way but one: The closet was too small. Big promised to build a bigger, better one, and Carrie was sold.

"I've died and gone to real estate heaven."

CARRIE

CARRIE WEARS THIS BELT, WHICH THE COSTUME DEPARTMENT NICK-NAMED "ROGER," MANY TIMES THROUGHOUT THE MOVIE...

...AS WELL AS THESE SHOES, DIOR EXTREMES

PATRICIA FIELD, COSTUME DESIGNER *I was really surprised by how much Sarah Jessica loved this belt. She's usually not so blown away by something that she refuses to take it off. She wears it several times in the movie, but it got to a point where I said, "You can't keep wearing the same thing every day!"*

On the way to Christie's auction house, Carrie told Miranda and Charlotte about her plans to move in with Big. Carrie had hoped they would be happy for her, but Miranda just seemed concerned that Carrie was taking a risk by giving up her own apartment.

"For now, can't you stop worrying for me and just go ahead and feel what I want you to feel—jealous?"

CARRIE

Inside Christie's, the girls were joined by Samantha, who had flown to New York to bid on a flower ring formerly owned by the actress Blair Elkenn.

"If 'schadenfreude'
is the word for
feeling pleasure at
someone else's misfortune,
this is 'jewelryfreude.'"

CARRIE

PATRICIA FIELD *The ring is a flower, and its stem extends beyond the fourth finger and sits on top of the pinky. I thought it was beautiful. I think it's worth about fifty thousand dollars.*

After an intense bidding war, Samantha drew the line at $50,000 and lost out to a mysterious phone bidder.

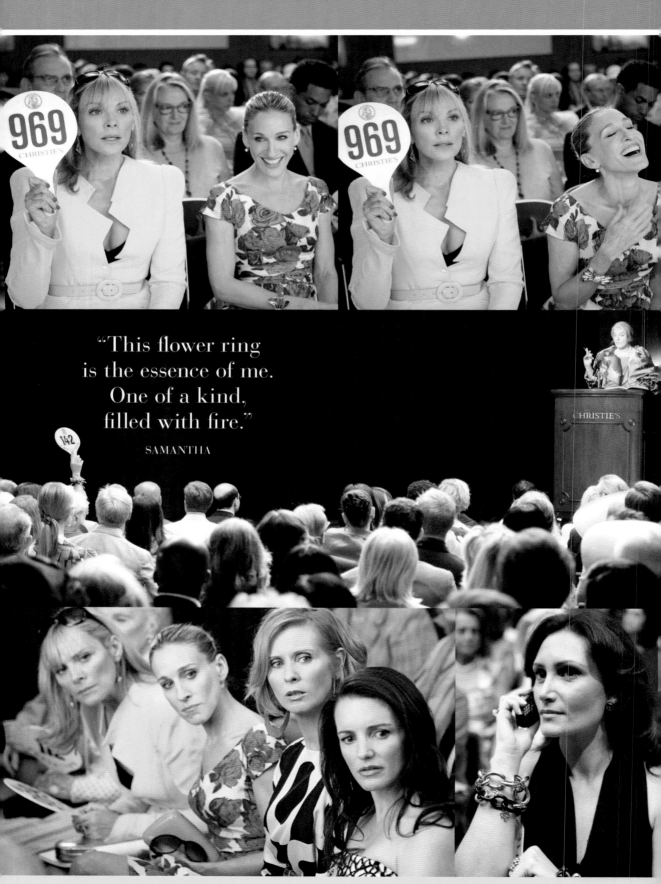

"This flower ring is the essence of me. One of a kind, filled with fire."

SAMANTHA

ERIC CYPHERS, CO-PRODUCER *Michael wanted the number on Samantha's bid paddle to be 69. Christie's didn't have a 69, but they did have a 969—a position I'm sure Samantha tried at least once in her life.*

In the ladies' room, after the auction, the girls overheard a woman talking about Blair's unfortunate situation. It seemed she'd trusted the wrong man to take care of her, and now she was left paying the price.

"She came home one night and he had locked her out. She didn't even have anywhere to live. After ten years. Such a shame. She was a smart girl till she fell in love."

That night, while Big cooked a lobster dinner, he and Carrie talked about whether she should sell her apartment. Carrie wanted to do it and put the money toward their new place. But Big had another thought: What if they were married?

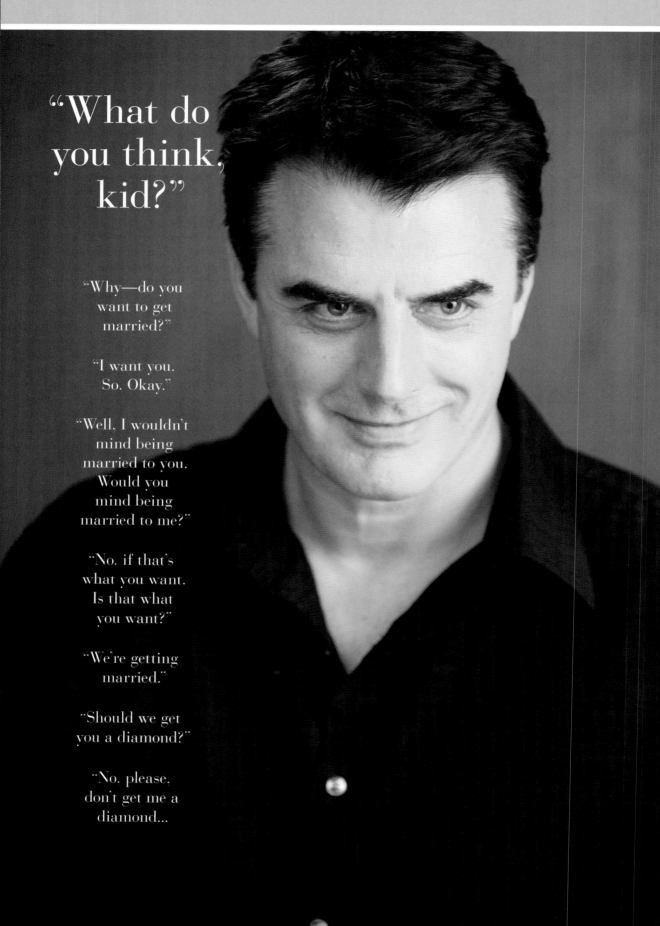

"What do you think, kid?"

"Why—do you want to get married?"

"I want you. So. Okay."

"Well, I wouldn't mind being married to you. Would you mind being married to me?"

"No, if that's what you want. Is that what you want?"

"We're getting married."

"Should we get you a diamond?"

"No, please, don't get me a diamond...

Before long, it was agreed: There would be a wedding in their future.

...get me a
really big
closet."

At brunch the next day, Carrie told Charlotte and Miranda that she and Big were getting married. Charlotte screamed, Miranda went deaf, and the entire restaurant broke out in applause.

"I'm sorry, but my friend here just got engaged, and she's been going out with the man for ten years."

CHARLOTTE

That afternoon, while shopping at Diane Von Furstenberg in the Meatpacking District, Carrie called Samantha to share the Big news. Samantha realized she would have to remove Carrie from her "we're never getting married" file.

"ROGER"
AGAIN

SARAH JESSICA PARKER *In one of the earliest fittings, Pat Field simply removed these shoes from her feet and ordered me to try them on. I willingly obliged.*

MICHAEL PATRICK KING *The first time you see Samantha's office, every inch of it is covered with pictures of Smith as a spokesperson for something. Our production designer, Jeremy Conway, did all that. Her life is all about Smith.*

At home with Charlotte and Anthony Marantino, Charlotte's former wedding planner, Carrie was excited to show off her wedding ensemble—a simple, off-white, label-less vintage suit—but her friends were less than impressed.

CARRIE'S PEN IS A PILOT VARSITY DISPOSABLE FOUNTAIN PEN

SARAH JESSICA PARKER *Carrie is a writer and always has a pen with her. The pen tucked into my dress is the same pen I always used in the series.*

"The bride wore a dress by no one."

ANTHONY

In the morning, Charlotte called Carrie with some exciting news: Her engagement to Big was mentioned in the *New York Post*'s gossip column, Page Six. Big, annoyed, wondered how they got the news.

Best-Seller Bliss

The ultimate single gal Carrie Bradshaw will be married in Manolos to New York financier John James Preston come fall, proving to single gals everywhere that there can be a happy ending over forty.

MICHAEL PATRICK KING *For the entire run of the show, we only knew Chris Noth's character by Carrie's nickname for him: Big. Finally, in the last episode, we learn that his name is John. I just thought, Why not? Make him John; make him everyman. But John is such a plain name, and I decided he needed something with more weight and class, so for the movie I gave him the full name John James Preston. I chose Preston in honor of Preston Sturges, a hugely important writer and director of romantic comedies.*

That same day, Carrie's editor Enid invited her to appear in *Vogue* magazine's "Age" issue as a forty-year-old bride. The article would feature Carrie dressed in a variety of stunning couture gowns. After some prodding from Enid, Carrie agreed.

"ROGER" THAT!

"Vogue designers,
Vogue photographers,
Vogue airbrushing.
Nod your head: yes."

ENID

SEX MEETS
VOGUE

One of the movie's most pivotal scenes occurs when Carrie is photographed in a series of stunning wedding gowns for *Vogue* magazine. It's a fun, over-the-top sequence that could only happen in the movies.

"From a writing point of view," explains Michael Patrick King, "I realized that having just one wedding gown in the movie wasn't going to do it. I wrote the *Vogue* montage, where she gets to wear a number of different dresses, so people could say, 'I like that one. No, I like that one.' Every dress is different for every woman."

But the fashion shoot couldn't have taken place at just any magazine. It had to be *Vogue* because, like Carrie, *Vogue* is iconic, stylish, and thoroughly New York. "I needed it to be the real *Vogue* magazine," King explains. "Consequently, the script had to be approved by [editor in chief] Anna Wintour."

To King's great relief, Wintour liked the script and surprised him by asking if he wanted the real *Vogue* creative team for Carrie's shoot. He told her he did, and she e-mailed him notes on the script. "She complimented me on what she liked and told me what she thought could be better, then closed her e-mail with, 'I hope you find these suggestions helpful—if not, throw them in the trash where they probably belong,'

HAIRSTYLIST
SERGE NORMANT

which I thought was incredibly classy."

Once Wintour was signed on, the *Vogue* staff began the arduous process of selecting the dresses. (It is the only scene in the film not fashion-directed by Patricia Field.) The *Sex and the City* crew met with Wintour and her staff over eight weeks to get approval for the gowns in the shoot. "I wanted the montage to be lush and dramatic in terms of design, but it also needed to seem real," says King. "There was a very limited amount of pre-production, so both camps really had to come together."

The day of the shoot was one of the most challenging for the cast, especially for Sarah Jessica Parker, who had to go through many difficult costume changes under harsh lights in short amounts of time. "We didn't even start shooting my scenes until two or three o'clock in the afternoon, and we had six or eight dresses to shoot," she says. "We had to change the scenery and lighting for each dress change."

Wintour also approved all of the *Vogue* background players in both the fashion shoot and the scenes at the *Vogue* offices. In the shoot, you can spot *Vogue* photographer Patrick Demarchelier, hairstylist Serge Normant, makeup artist Gucci Westman, prop stylist Mary Howard, West Coast edi-

tor Lawren Howell, contributing editor Plum Sykes, and editor-at-large André Leon Talley.

In addition to providing a memorable cameo, Talley served two important functions on set: He ensured that everything was authentic, and he coached Parker on how to pose. "The dress that was most physically cumbersome was the Dior dress with the massive hat," she recalls. "It was really tight at the waist, and required that I stand the way that those models did in the fifties, where you contort your body and go concave. André directed me to stand that way. I happily obliged."

Talley had initially said he could stay at the shoot only until five o'clock, but he wound up staying until the middle of the night, when the crew wrapped. Parker, who has done several real shoots for *Vogue*, found this one similar to the real thing, except "André was never at any of my shoots. It was like having the Godfather come to dinner. He scrutinized everything with an eagle's eye, which you've no idea how much Michael and I appreciated."

There was one dress that the costume department was unable to gain access to for the shoot. Molly Rogers had seen a picture of an Yves Saint Laurent dress from his 2002 retrospective. The

VOGUE EDITOR-AT-LARGE ANDRÉ LEON TALLEY

ANDRÉ LEON TALLEY

dress (nicknamed "the Q-Tip") was similar in shape to a giant ice-cream cone, and it created a dome over the entire body, with just a hole for the face to peek out and two holes for the hands. Recalls associate producer Melinda Relyea, "Michael had this hysterical idea that Carrie would be in this priceless piece of fragile, white couture that she could barely move in, and she would begin hopping over to the craft-services table for food or a glass of red wine, which would send all the assistants running to stop her. However, the dress was actually from a collection in the '60s, and was with the Yves Saint Laurent Foundation in Paris. We tried everything we could think of to access the dress—we called the Metropolitan Museum of Art's Costume Institute, friends of Yves Saint Laurent, and the Foundation itself. We had a plan that we would fly the dress in with handlers, who would only remove it from its box for the time we needed it for the shoot. Sadly, none of our plans were convincing enough to the Foundation, and the dress stayed in France."

In the end, there is only one dress with which Carrie falls in love—the Vivienne Westwood. After the shoot, Westwood sends Carrie the dress as a gift, and the rest, of course, is movie history.

CHRISTIAN LACROIX

CHRISTIAN DIOR

LANVIN

"A dress so special,
it could wring a
wedding tear from
even the most
unbelieving of women."

CARRIE

VIVIENNE WESTWOOD

Back at Carrie's apartment, a deliveryman arrived with a large dress box containing the Vivienne Westwood wedding gown, a gift from the designer herself. Carrie was floored.

VIVIENNE WESTWOOD PENNED THIS NOTE FOR THE MOVIE

Vivienne Westwood

Dear Carrie,
I saw your photo from the Vogue shoot. This dress belongs to you!
♡
Vivienne Westwood

MICHAEL PATRICK KING *I loved the idea that the wedding gown comes from Vivenne Westwood. It's perfect—if you follow the Cinderella thread throughout the movie. It's the fairy godmother, a colorful, outrageous older woman, who gives Cinderella the dress. Come on—how Vivienne Westwood is that?*

"And just like that, Vivienne Westwood kicked my sweet little suit's ass."

After spending a romantic evening with him, Carrie read aloud to Big from *The Love Letters of Great Men: Volume One*. Big admitted that love letters weren't his style—but that didn't mean he didn't care for Carrie.

"You make me
very happy."

BIG

MICHAEL PATRICK KING *Carrie and Big's bed scene is interesting because it's the best, idealized version of them. His shirt is open, he's in teal pajamas, he's in good shape. She's in a sexy chemise, wearing pearls. If they had only just stayed there and not tried to get married, they would have lived happily ever after. When they're reading in bed, Carrie borrows his glasses. She refuses to acknowledge that she can't see—both literally and figuratively. Only later, after she's been jilted, does she realize she hadn't wanted to see what was happening.*

"Yeah, yeah…
put it in writing."
CARRIE

Be calm—love me—
today—yesterday—
what tearful longings for
you—you—you—
my life—my all—farewell.
Oh continue to love me—
never misjudge
the most faithful heart
of your beloved.
Ever thine,
ever mine,
ever ours.

LUDWIG VAN BEETHOVEN

MEI LAI HIPPISLEY-COXE, COSTUMER *For this scene, Patricia Field had dressed Sarah Jessica Parker in a T-shirt and leggings. But Michael Patrick King was concerned that Big and Carrie looked too comfortable. It was important to show the contrast between Steve and Miranda, who weren't having sex, and Carrie and Big, who were.*

The next day, while returning some books to the New York Public Library, Carrie saw a deliveryman carrying an arrangement of flowers into the building. Intrigued, she followed him and found a beautifully decorated wedding space—which gave her an idea.

MOLLY ROGERS, COSTUME DESIGNER *Carrie's dressed in Proenza Schouler, which is a small fashion house, so they had only one sample. We used it once, but when we needed it again they sent us the wrong shoes and the wrong vest. Finally, we got the right outfit and raced it to Sarah Jessica's trailer—just in time.*

SARAH JESSICA PARKER ISN'T WEARING ANY MASCARA IN THIS SCENE

CARRIE NEVER ACTUALLY WEARS THE HAT SHE'S CARRYING IN THIS SCENE– BECAUSE IT WOULDN'T FIT OVER HER BUN

ERIC CYPHERS *The New York Public Library and its "backyard," Bryant Park, was our home for four days while shooting the whole wedding sequence. There must be a million people who work in this part of town, and during lunchtime at least half of them came to watch. None of us had ever seen crowds like that.*

At dinner in Brooklyn, Miranda felt criticized when Steve lightheartedly pointed out some cappuccino foam on her lip. Later that night, they made love for the first time in months, but Miranda uttered something regrettable: "Let's just get it over with."

MICHAEL PATRICK KING *It's amazing that in a rocky relationship scene like this the real challenge was the cappuccino foam. Getting the right thickness and texture was a nightmare for the props department—too thick, too thin, juuust right—a real Goldilocks syndrome. Aside from her amazing emotional work in this scene, Cynthia Nixon was a technical master when it came to sticking her nose in the cup at just the right angle to get enough foam on her lip.*

ERIC CYPHERS *Poor Joe Pupo, who plays Brady—he must have eaten a pound of spaghetti during this scene. We thought he was going to explode, but his mom later told me that he was still hungry that night after filming and asked to stop for pizza on the way home.*

The next morning, over breakfast with the girls and Lily, Miranda confessed that she and Steve hadn't had sex in six months, which led to a colorful discussion of their sex lives (in code for Lily's sake).

CYNTHIA NIXON *For the show, we always shot the coffee shop scenes at Silvercup Studios, but for the movie the producers rented an empty store in SoHo and re-created it. It was so freaky because it felt fake. They even rented some stores across the street to match the backdrop of the original coffee shop. Our set had grown up enough to wander out into the real world. It was like Pinocchio—the coffee shop is a real boy!*

MICHAEL PATRICK KING *When Carrie is coloring in the Cinderella book, she's coloring Cinderella's shoe blue, which is a reference to the Manolo that Big places on Carrie's foot at the end of the movie.*

Carrie felt thankful that she and Big—even after all their years together—still had a passionate relationship.

"When Big colors, he rarely stays in the lines."
CARRIE

In L.A., Samantha learned that Smith was the mystery bidder on the petal ring—a fifth-anniversary gift. But when she tried to thank him with a night of hot sex, he said he needed to sleep. Instead, she was treated to the sounds of her neighbor having hot sex.

"To be clear,
this is a ring with
diamonds—
not a diamond ring,
right?"

SAMANTHA

Up at the Fifth Avenue penthouse, Big was finally ready to reveal the new, improved closet to Carrie. With double doors and shelves upon shelves for shoes, it was love at first sight. Carrie decided to try it out and placed her blue Manolos on the shelf.

THIS PURSE—
AN HERMÈS LOAN—
HAD TO BE RETURNED
AS SOON AS FILMING
WAS OVER FOR
THE DAY

MICHAEL PATRICK KING *The closet is like candy. I wanted the audience to gasp when Big reveals it. It is a gesture of extravagance, a perfect expression of Big's love for Carrie. It may not be a typical expression—like an engagement ring—but it shows that he knows what's really important to her.*

SARAH JESSICA PARKER WAS AT A FITTING IN THESE CLOTHES, AND PATRICIA FIELD SUGGESTED SHE WEAR THEM FOR THIS SCENE

MICHAEL PATRICK KING *Sarah Jessica, Patricia Field, and I had a huge discussion about using Manolo Blahniks in this scene: "What does it mean if Carrie's still buying Manolos?" Manolo is a flashpoint of emotion for Carrie and her fans, and this is the first time in the movie we see them.*

But moving her wardrobe into a new closet meant clearing out her old one, so, back at Carrie's apartment, Miranda, Charlotte, Samantha, and Lily helped Carrie decide what she should take—and what she should toss.

MICHAEL PATRICK KING *This was a magical night on the movie set. It was standing-room only around the video monitor as the actresses charged down the closet runway. At the end of the shoot, there was a huge round of applause for the girls and our amazing junior wardrobe designers, Paolo Nieddu and Jessica Replansky, who combed every Goodwill and vintage shop in New York City to find these amazing and iconically ridiculous clothes.*

THE TUTU IS THE
ONLY OUTFIT THAT THEY
ALL SAY TO "TAKE"

MELINDA RELYEA, ASSOCIATE PRODUCER *If you look closely at Carrie's closet in the background of this scene, you can find many iconic pieces Carrie wore on the show—like the green tutu she wore in Paris.*

Finally, her apartment empty, Carrie said good-bye for one last time.

"It took four friends three days to put twenty years into thirty-eight boxes."

CARRIE

Later, in Brooklyn, Miranda and Steve sat in their kitchen trying to figure out how to juggle the next day's busy schedule. Seemingly out of nowhere, Steve burst into tears, confessing to Miranda that he had cheated on her.

"I had sex with someone else."

STEVE

Stunned, Miranda walked out, taking Brady with her.

Against her better instincts, Miranda went home the next night, but when she saw Steve, she knew she couldn't stay—so she moved into the Mercer Hotel. In the morning, over brunch with the girls, Miranda said she didn't think she could ever forgive Steve.

JOHN MELFI, PRODUCER *We had been wanting to shoot at the Mercer Hotel for years, so we were thrilled when owner Andre Balazs finally let us. And chef Jean-Georges Vongerichten let us shoot inside the hotel's restaurant, Mercer Kitchen.*

CYNTHIA NIXON *Joseph Pupo plays Brady. He is so tremendous. He is such a unique person and looks so astonishingly like both me and David Eigenberg. He's a very un-Hollywood kid, and you can tell he's got a lot going on in his mind. He really lights up the screen. All the actors feel protective when there are kids or babies on the set, but Sarah and I, having been child actors ourselves, feel a heightened sense of responsibility.*

When Carrie and Big reviewed their ballooning guest list, Carrie joked that her dress had upped the ante. But Big wasn't amused. He admitted he'd rather get married at City Hall. Sensing her devastation, Big rushed to apologize, and all was forgiven.

"It's a circus!
Two hundred people,
Page Six! This is my
third marriage.
How do you think it
makes me look?"

BIG

MELINDA RELYEA *After this scene was shot, we needed to do a reshoot, but the wardrobe department learned that Carrie's tie-dyed dress was being used in a Vogue photo shoot in the Mayan jungle. A wardrobe assistant had to fly to Mexico, pick it up, and come right back. She had a margarita at the airport.*

At their engagement party at Buddakan, the night before the wedding, Big and Carrie endured some unkind words from Big's coworker, Karl, who mocked the fact that Big had been married twice before.

"You know what they say— three times a charm!"

KARL

"Here's to the groom— a man who finally got 'Carrie-d' away."

SAMANTHA

JOHN MELFI *The Buddakan shoot was epic—it took three days. The table sat thirty-six people, and all of Carrie and Big's friends had to look believable. Michael Patrick King loved the staircase in Buddakan, and we were really able to take advantage of it with a beautiful overhead crane shot.*

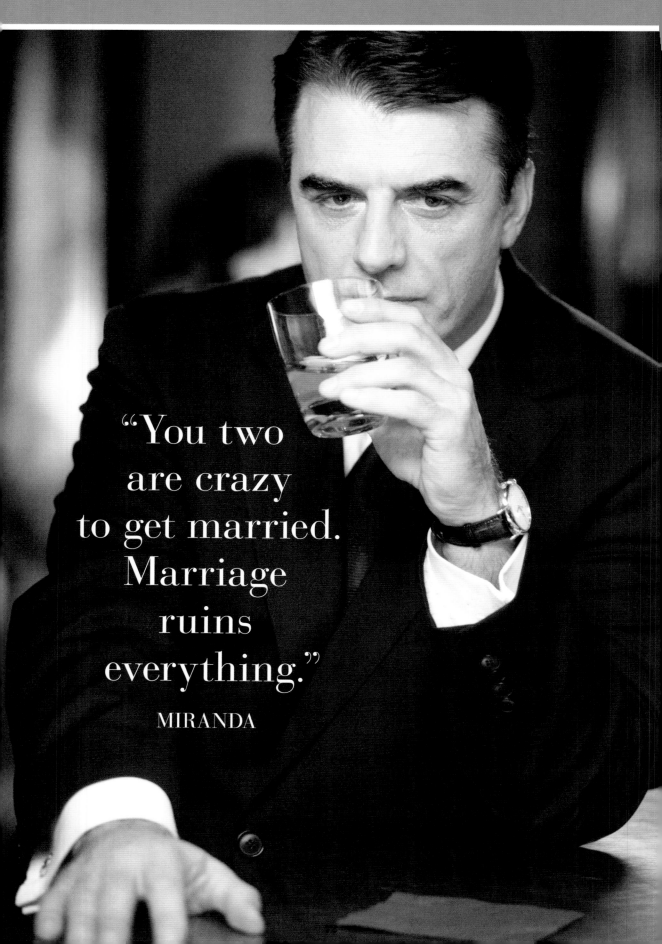

Outside the restaurant, as Samantha smoked cigars with Big, Harry, and Smith, Steve showed up unexpectedly, hoping to speak with Miranda. She agreed to hear him out, and he begged for her forgiveness.

"You two are crazy to get married. Marriage ruins everything."

MIRANDA

Miranda stormed back inside and told Big he was a fool to be getting married. More nervous than ever, Big asked Carrie to spend the night with him, but she wouldn't cancel her plans for an all-gal sleepover. Instead, she gave him one last single-girl kiss.

MICHAEL PATRICK KING *John Thomas, our director of photography, is a master of contrasting light and dark. You can see it in the deep textures and colors in this shot. At Buddakan, he made a dinner table set for thirty-six look like something out of the Renaissance. Many times when I was looking at his work, I felt like I was looking at a painting.*

That night, the four women (and Lily) gathered in Charlotte's bedroom. But their girl talk was interrupted by a phone call from Big, who confessed to Carrie that he was worried about screwing things up.

"There we sat, like a scene out of Louisa May Alcott's *Not-So-Little Women*."

CARRIE

MICHAEL PATRICK KING *The impossible dream was to find an actress magical enough to play Lily, who could say the word "sex" on cue in this scene. To help Allie Fong, Sarah Jessica and Kristin played a little acting game with her. They would squeeze her leg under the covers, and that would be her cue to say "sex." After one or two takes, Allie no longer needed their help. She got it . . . BIG time.*

"This is me that you're marrying tomorrow. Me. Nobody else... And you want to know the good news there? We've already both done everything we can to screw it up."

CARRIE

Carrie, sensing a case of slightly cold feet, reassured him that there was no need to be nervous. But when she tried to get some sleep later on, she couldn't help but worry.

SARAH JESSICA PARKER *We deliberately chose to stick with the pink phone Carrie had at the end of the series. Carrie is not a phone person, so I asked our props department to break off a bunch of the Swarovski crystals and then duct tape it to make it look barely held together.*

In the morning, Carrie dressed for her wedding, and everyone agreed she looked stunning.

THE COSTUME DEPARTMENT NICK-NAMED CHARLOTTE'S ZAC POSEN DRESS "THE BLACK SWAN"

Meanwhile, Big was still feeling anxious and tried to call Carrie—only to be hung up on by Lily. Unaware that Big was trying to reach her, Carrie headed to the library with the wedding party.

KRISTIN DAVIS *The twins who play Lily, Allie and Parker Fong, were a lot of fun and so professional. I always had a fantastic time with them in the hair and makeup trailer. My biggest problem was trying to stop myself from playing with their hair during my scenes with them. They were perfect!*

Outside the library, Big waited for Carrie to arrive, hoping to talk to her before the ceremony, but when her car pulled up and she emerged, Charlotte rushed her inside, pulling the veil over her face.

THESE
DIOR EXTREME
SHOES WERE
COVERED IN
SMOKE- AND
OYSTER-COLORED
CRYSTALS

MICHAEL PATRICK KING
*For the bridesmaids'
dresses, we initially
wanted a kind of uni-
form—they were all go-
ing to be red. When Pat
came up with this color
scheme—and I saw them
in the gray and marble
library—the colors really
popped. Those dresses
never got boring.*

When Big finally spotted his Carrie, all he could see was a bride.

"I need to know
that it's still us.
Just like you said.
Me and you."

As the girls rushed inside, Stanford explained that Big was nowhere to be found. Panicked, Carrie grabbed a phone and called him, only to be hit with the terrible news: He couldn't go through with it.

"I can't do this."

BIG

MICHAEL PATRICK KING *Here's the thing about Sarah Jessica Parker's performance in the movie: It can't be called acting. It's more like watching someone living in front of a camera. She's breathing and feeling and being Carrie Bradshaw.*

CYNTHIA NIXON *It was great to shoot in the library. It's so beautiful, and to be there at off hours and feel like it's your place is amazing. Because we were in those gowns, we didn't want to dress outside. They gave us the most beautiful room I've ever seen as our dressing room, with tapestries of the continents on the walls.*

Devastated, she told the girls the wedding was off. Charlotte and Miranda whisked her away while Samantha stayed to deal with the guests.

MICHAEL PATRICK KING *For Carrie's wedding dress, we were looking for something with a Cinderella quality. I wanted her to look really hung out and jilted in it—all dressed up and nowhere to go. When Carrie runs down the library stairs, there's no Prince Charming chasing after her.*

Moments later, realizing he was making a huge mistake, Big chased down Carrie and told her he was ready—that he had just lost his nerve. But it was too late. Carrie, wounded, attacked him with her bouquet as onlookers gaped at the spectacle.

"You left! I am humiliated!"

CARRIE

SARAH JESSICA PARKER *To see Kristin and Cynthia's faces was startling to me. Charlotte is holding Carrie, and Charlotte screams at Big, "No!" When I was learning my lines, I was thinking about the beats and the blocking, but I didn't think about how they would play it. They were a wreck. No one realized how upsetting this movie was going to be. But it's okay. It doesn't have to be candy all the time. It's about how to rely on each other and what happens when nobody can fix things.*

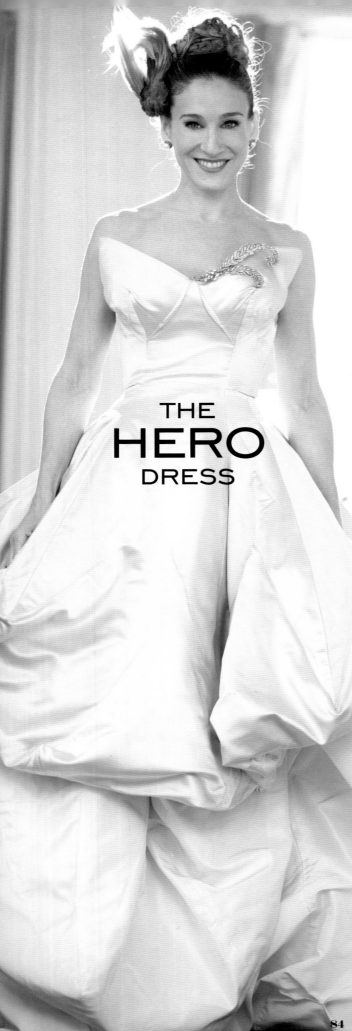

THE HERO DRESS

In the movie-production world, the word "hero" is used to describe a wardrobe item that must be kept intact no matter what happens in a scene. Usually a duplicate version of the hero is created that can be mussed, while the hero version is used only for scenes that don't involve stunts.

But Carrie's Vivienne Westwood wedding gown is a hero dress in both senses of the word. Because there was no duplicate, the dress was used in ways it probably shouldn't have. And it was a metaphorical hero in terms of the magic and possibility it represented to Carrie. The dress could also be said to be the cause of her downfall, because it signifies a wedding that spun out of control.

Costume designers Patricia Field and Molly Rogers, along with Danny Santiago and Paolo Nieddu, began looking at wedding dresses in July 2007. Writer and director Michael Patrick King felt it was important that the dress have a ball-like, Cinderella quality. At the same time, the gown had to be right for Carrie, who is known for her iconoclastic fashion sense. The team ended up looking at everything from a cherry blossom–print dress off the rack from Kleinfeld (a New York bridal institution) to a Haitian wedding gown with a twenty-eight-foot train. Like Prince Charming searching for Cinderella, they felt they would know they had the right gown when they saw it.

Rogers, for her part, had been hoping to get a Christian Dior gown with a huge flower on it that she had seen at a show in Paris. DVDs were sent to Bernard Arnault, the head of LVMH, which owns Dior, but ultimately the dress did not materialize. Rogers was disappointed: "In an earlier version of the script, the gown had to show up in the fashion show after the wedding. So this gown was going to dictate which designer's fashion show was in the movie. The biggest bang for the buck would have been a Dior show, because Dior is known for being completely theatrical."

Field, on the other hand, fell in love with a Zac Posen dress that Charlotte ultimately wears (in black) as a bridesmaid dress. "It's sexy, and it's more appropriate for Carrie," says Field. "It came down to the Posen dress redone in white and the Vivienne Westwood. But the Westwood was always in the running because of its volume. The wedding reels out of control, so the dress was story-appropriate."

"When we were looking for the dress," Sarah Jessica Parker recalls, "Michael Patrick said, 'What is the dress that Carrie never would have dreamed about for her wedding but that, when she pulls it out of the box, turns her into a seven-year-old girl?' To me, that was the Westwood."

When Parker tried on the dress, she loved

its combination of traditional and edgy elements. "Other designers are conventionally more beautiful but aren't subversive," she says. "The dress has a strange bustline that stands away from the body, and it's two or three times larger than any woman's natural bustline would be. At the same time, it's not too eccentric, and it has the fairy-tale quality we were looking for, due to all that volume. Because Big has to see Carrie as a perfect bride, she couldn't be wearing some crazy outfit, which she's prone to doing."

Once the dress was selected, the costume department had to contend with the matter of the veil. "The veil was essential to the story," explains King. "I kept saying to Pat, 'What's happening with the veil?' but the costume department was being very cagey about it."

During Parker's first fitting, there was a table with vintage jewelry and hats on it. She spotted the bird among them. "I said, 'What is that? We have to find a place for that bird.' We tried it during different fittings and it didn't work with anything, but I kept pushing for it. When I first tried on the Vivienne Westwood dress in my trailer, Danny brought that bird along, and all of a sudden it made sense."

The day the wedding scene was to be shot, only a few minutes before Carrie was to appear in the veil, the costume department told King that they were ready for him to see it. "I walked in and saw that blue bird," he remembers, "and I completely shut down. It was a big choice. I didn't want to react, so I got out of the room before I said anything."

"Michael looked like someone had punched him," says Parker. "I could tell that he was trying to remain calm and not deflate our excitement over this bird. He said, 'I'm just going to take a minute. Is that a bird on your head?' I said, 'It's a bird on my head.'"

King left the room and thought about it for a while. Finally, he went back in to take another look. "When Sarah Jessica looked up at me with her blue eyes under that blue bird, I was sold," he says.

The wedding scene was one of the most challenging of the movie to shoot, largely because of the dress. It required two costume dressers, and because it had to be used in the street, the costume department created an inner tube to put inside it so it wouldn't drag. Carrie's wedding shoes are Dior Extreme sandals dipped in Swarovski crystals. The bridesmaid dresses are all Zac Posen samples. Luckily, the three actresses fit into them.

In typical *Sex and the City* style, the Westwood dress has already garnered a fan base of its own. Two "hero-worshipping" brides had ordered it by the time the movie wrapped. The cost: $25,000.

That night, the girls did their best to comfort Carrie, but all she could think about was the honeymoon she'd have to cancel. Determined not to let a good vacation go to waste, Samantha decided that they should all go to Mexico together.

"I had gone from *Little Women* to *Little Drunk Women*."

CARRIE

When they arrived, Charlotte and Miranda saw the romantic, rose-covered honeymoon suite and hurriedly swept away the evidence. Carrie promptly collapsed into the bed—and sank into a Mexicoma.

SARAH JESSICA PARKER *I begged Michael to let me bring the muff. I thought, What would Carrie have packed to travel with her new husband? Everything she wears in Mexico would have been packed for her honeymoon, which made it all the more depressing.*

ERIC CYPHERS *The golf-cart scene made us nervous. During Season Three of the show, the girls went to Los Angeles, and they all piled into Carrie's rented vintage Mustang convertible. Unfortunately, it had vintage brakes to match, and they gave out on a hillside while all the girls were in the car. It was terrifying, but thankfully no one was hurt. So, for this scene, we put five burly teamsters in the cart and ran them up and down the hill a few times—just to ease our minds. That old Mustang was the first thing that popped into our heads when we saw this hill.*

While Carrie slept, Charlotte, Samantha, and Miranda ate lunch on the patio. Charlotte snacked on a package of pudding (from Poughkeepsie) because it was the only thing she felt safe eating in Mexico.

CYNTHIA NIXON *The challenge for us about the Mexico shoot was the temperature. It was pretty cold, and we were on the side of a cliff, so the wind was very extreme—and we're all in bathing suits. As cold as it is on a New York City street in a skimpy gown and heels, it's much worse lying there in a bathing suit in California, not even moving but pretending to be luxuriating in the sun.*

JOHN MELFI *We shot the Mexico scenes in the mountains north of Malibu, at a compound that had the most extraordinary views. It looks like it could be Mexico or Capri. We had the opportunity to shoot in the Caribbean for free, but we had to keep it in Mexico for the "Mexicoma" joke.*

Later that afternoon, while the girls were sunbathing, Samantha got an eyeful of the national forest growing between Miranda's legs.

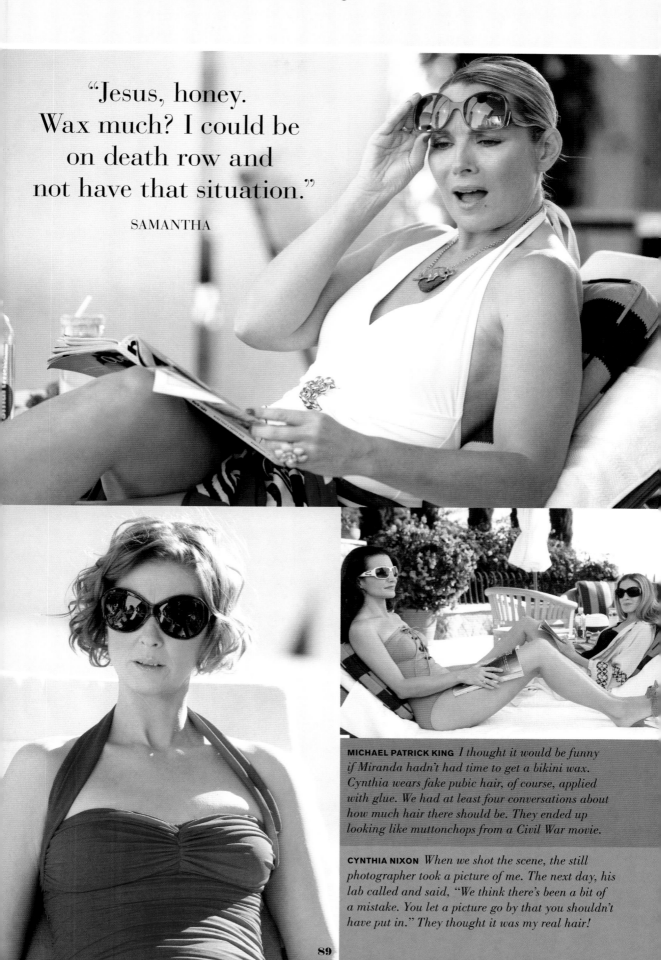

"Jesus, honey. Wax much? I could be on death row and not have that situation."

SAMANTHA

MICHAEL PATRICK KING *I thought it would be funny if Miranda hadn't had time to get a bikini wax. Cynthia wears fake pubic hair, of course, applied with glue. We had at least four conversations about how much hair there should be. They ended up looking like muttonchops from a Civil War movie.*

CYNTHIA NIXON *When we shot the scene, the still photographer took a picture of me. The next day, his lab called and said, "We think there's been a bit of a mistake. You let a picture go by that you shouldn't have put in." They thought it was my real hair!*

When Carrie finally awoke, the girls convinced her to go out for dinner. Over drinks, Carrie mused about her fate, wondering if she would ever laugh again. Miranda assured her that she would, the next time something was really, really funny.

MICHAEL PATRICK KING *In the Mexico sequence, I initially had Carrie taking full responsibility for what happened to her, but then I decided she wouldn't have come to that understanding the day after being jilted. So instead I turned it into a "we hate men" scene. There needed to be an element of margaritas and fun, but without taking it to a Girls Gone Wild level.*

SARAH JESSICA PARKER *When we filmed these scenes, it was 2 a.m. or thereabouts and pouring rain, and Christmas was imminent. But we seemed as far away from Christmas as is possible, there in Simi Valley. We were outside getting some air—me and other members of the crew—and we started singing songs, one of my favorite ways to pass time when the hours are late. And then it just turned into Christmas carols. We were exhausted and singing as loud as our lungs would allow, and people came out from the set and laughed and smiled. We weren't wonderful, but it was such great fun, and it was immensely memorable and got us through that night.*

"After everything I know, after twenty years of everything we've learned, I threw it all away for the thrill of putting his name on the honeymoon suite. If I met me now, I wouldn't know me."

CARRIE

In the shower, while picturing her loved ones in New York, Charlotte forgot for a moment that she was in Mexico—and drank the water. Then Charlotte "Poughkeepsied" in her pants.

MICHAEL PATRICK KING *When Kristin found out that Charlotte was going to "Poughkeepsie" in her pants, she said, "Oh, my God, Michael." But I said, "It's funny."*

And, for the first time since the wedding that never was, Carrie laughed.

KRISTIN DAVIS *This scene was a big concern for me, because what happens to Charlotte is so embarrassing. But I discussed it with Michael Patrick King, and he reassured me that it would be funny and not gross. I just had to trust him.*

At the end of the trip, finally ready to face her "mailbox full" alert, Carrie checked her messages. But when she heard Big's voice, she impulsively threw her phone off a cliff.

After returning to New York—and an apartment cluttered with boxes and wedding gifts—Carrie decided she needed to hire an assistant. But none of the applicants she interviewed was quite right . . .

. . . except Louise from St. Louis, who had moved to New York to find love.

MICHAEL PATRICK KING *This scene was filmed at a Starbucks on Astor Place, but it may as well have been on Broadway. All four actors who play the assistants—including Oscar-winning Dreamgirl Jennifer Hudson—are amazing singers from Broadway and the club circuit. This was Jennifer's first day working on the movie, and at the end of the night (with a little gentle prodding) she treated the cast and crew to an a cappella version of "And I Am Telling You I'm Not Going." And, I am telling you, we were delighted.*

While Louise organized Carrie's old apartment, Miranda set out to find a new one, back in Manhattan. She, Magda, and Brady happened upon the perfect place— a building on the Lower East Side, just on the other side of the Brooklyn Bridge.

ERIC CYPHERS *It was pretty colorful shooting on the Lower East Side. Most people in New York dread a noisy, invasive film crew, but the locals were very hospitable. We made snow that night and all the neighborhood kids came out to play in it—they'd never seen anything like it before.*

With her cell phone floating somewhere in the Pacific Ocean, Carrie was forced to call Samantha from a pay phone. She told her friend she wasn't quite ready to reconnect to the world.

Phone

"No phone,
no calls.
No calls,
no questions.
No questions,
no explaining
no wedding."

CARRIE

PATRICIA FIELD *Carrie is famous for mixing different pieces together. A good example is the outfit she wears when she's on the pay phone. It's a really short T-shirt dress from my store, with an off-the-shoulder sweater, a Prada handbag, and a half glove. When I saw Sarah Jessica in it at the fitting, I screamed, "Carrie's back!"*

And even though she still had no phone to her name, Carrie couldn't escape an e-mail from Big. So Louise filed his e-mails in a folder, blocking them from Carrie's inbox.

"Isn't there some
cyberspace place
that you can send those
so that I never have
to see an e-mail
from him ever again?"
CARRIE

A few days later, Carrie found herself reading *Cinderella* to Lily and felt compelled to explain that it was only a fairy tale. Unfortunately, Carrie's editorializing proved useless—Lily was hooked.

"This is a fairy tale, sweetheart. Things don't always happen like this in real life. You should know that now."

CARRIE

THESE ARE SARAH JESSICA PARKER'S FAVORITE "CARRIE" JEANS

MICHAEL PATRICK KING *There is an old showbiz rule: Never work with children or small animals. Well, unless you're Kristin Davis. She was amazing with Allie and Parker, the twins who play Lily, and she always had time to cuddle with the three dogs—both on and off the set.*

When Charlotte returned home from her trip to the doctor's office, she had some exciting news: She was pregnant. Carrie was delighted by the reminder that, in certain houses, fairy tales do come true.

"My doctor said sometimes when women stop trying, it can happen."

CHARLOTTE

ERIC CYPHERS *Penny, who plays Elizabeth Taylor, Charlotte's King Charles Spaniel, came out of retirement for the movie. The puppies aren't the originals from the series, though. We had to put makeup on the new dogs to make the spots around their eyes match those of the dogs on the series.*

In the fall, while the two shopped for Halloween costumes, Carrie told Miranda about the e-mail Big had sent her, and Miranda revealed that Steve couldn't stop apologizing. Then Carrie spotted *Vogue* and read the article she knew would haunt her forever.

"ROGER,"
YET AGAIN

"That's it? The only two choices for women: witch and sexy kitten."
MIRANDA

To help get Carrie's mind off the past—and *Vogue*—Charlotte and Lily invited her to join them for a night of trick-or-treating. But Carrie couldn't knock on a single door without being recognized from the article. She was mortified. . . .

"I'm the scariest thing in New York: jilted at forty-one. Boo!"
CARRIE

MICHAEL PATRICK KING *We had to create the Cinderella mask ourselves, and I wanted her to be blond because so often girls choose the blond-haired fantasy despite their background.*

MICHAEL PATRICK KING *We had a discussion on set before we shot the dog in this rabbi costume. Politically incorrect? Or funny? Or both? In the end, it made us laugh a lot, so we erred on the side of funny.*

> "My head is in the
> witness protection program."
> CARRIE

SARAH JESSICA PARKER *My wig was created by a great wigmaker here in New York named Martial Corneville. During filming, I'd have to keep switching back and forth between the wig and my natural hair. In order to put it on, it had to be "wrapped," a complicated technique where one's own hair is molded as flat as possible to her head. Mandy Lyons, my hairstylist, became an expert!*

A BRIEF
HISTORY
OF
CARRIE'S
HAIR

Later that day, Louise gave Carrie a new cell phone—with a 347 area code. Carrie was extremely disappointed, having always considered herself a 917 girl.

"I want the old New York, with the old 917 and my old will to live."

CARRIE

MICHAEL PATRICK KING *The brown hair signifies a journey away from the girl Carrie was—a dark period. Patricia Field put Sarah Jessica in dark clothes throughout this entire segment of the movie. Carrie is like a tree that has lost its foliage. She hibernates, goes underground.*

Out in L.A., Samantha went shopping to get out of the house—and away from the temptation of her "sex on a stick" neighbor. She passed a dog-rescue station and glimpsed a tiny, tattered dog—all alone.

JOHN MELFI *We auditioned only two dogs for the role of Samantha's dog, and the one that we ended up choosing, Gidget, had to come back twice, and at different times of the day, so we could make sure she could hump on cue. She's a star.*

KIM CATTRALL *I've never really worked with animals, and now I know why. Gidget was the biggest star on the set because she got to go home first. But I love that Samantha finds this mutt that needs love and care. Her life involves family, and I like what the dog represents for her character.*

Sensing something special about it, Samantha decided to adopt it.

At night, while unpacking clothes with Louise, Carrie discovered her wedding gown. Louise offered to get rid of it, but Carrie wouldn't let her, confessing that she still missed Big. Louise admitted that she still missed her ex, too.

"I'll just bury it deep
in the back—
like I did my feelings."

CARRIE

SARAH JESSICA PARKER *I think people are going to be surprised that the second act of the movie, and a bit of the third act, are incredibly sad. It's a real, grown-up story. For Big to disappoint Carrie the way he does is beyond reckoning. It's one thing to be in your early thirties and have to ask yourself, Why am I not the person? But it's another to find oneself left at the altar. What happens to Carrie is very painful. People aren't expecting that from this movie.*

Realizing that two broken hearts were too many for one walk-in closet, Carrie and Louise went out for cocktails. Louise told Carrie that even though it hurt to know her ex didn't think she was "the one," she wasn't going to give up on love.

"See that?
I'm bringing it to me
all day long."
LOUISE

Love

JOHN MELFI *For the scene where Carrie and Louise go out for drinks, we shot in Bemelmans Bar at the Carlyle hotel. No one had ever shot there before.*

JENNIFER HUDSON *When Sarah and I were shooting the scene at Bemelmans, she told me about Bobby Short. I said, "Who?" She said, "You're too young to know about him," and she gave me one of his CDs.*

A few days later, when Harry asked Charlotte why she hadn't been running like usual, she snapped at him.

MICHAEL PATRICK KING *Charlotte worked really hard to find happiness, so I always knew that her story line was going to be, "I'm so happy, I'm terrified." She feels guilty that she's happy and her friends aren't.*

Charlotte confessed to Carrie that even though the doctor had said it was fine for her to run, she was convinced something bad was going to happen to her.

"I've got everything
I ever wanted.
I'm so happy,
I'm terrified."

CHARLOTTE

SARAH JESSICA PARKER *I'm wearing an Yves Saint Laurent outfit in this scene, and the people from YSL were literally standing by the wardrobe truck waiting for me to take it off so they could take it back to Paris.*

Fall came and went. Before Louise headed back to St. Louis for Christmas, Carrie gave her a Louis Vuitton purse, which she would no longer have to "bag, borrow, or steal," and Louise gave Carrie a copy of *Meet Me in St. Louis*.

SARAH JESSICA PARKER *Jennifer Hudson is lovely, and she surprised me in this movie. First of all, she's very pretty; in* Dreamgirls *she doesn't get to be the pretty one. She's tall, and she has a beautiful face and beautiful skin. There's a maternal quality about her that's so important to the story. A lot of the change that happens to Carrie is put in place by her character. The scene where I say goodbye to Louise was so hard.*

JENNIFER HUDSON *In real life, I am a bag person. I love bags. When we were filming in New York, I had all my designer bags there with me, and one day Sarah Jessica thought the bag I was carrying with me was from Louise's wardrobe. It wasn't! I don't have this Vuitton bag, but I want it.*

On New Year's Eve, Carrie tried to write, but all she could come up with was the word "love"—and an ellipsis. Soon, she fell asleep. Downtown, Steve stopped by to pick up Brady, and despite his best efforts, left Miranda behind to celebrate alone.

MICHAEL PATRICK KING *Carrie's home has become a kind of shrine. Women and girls, married and single, come here to sit on the stoop and be Carrie—just for a moment. We owe a huge debt of gratitude to the residents of Perry Street in historic Greenwich Village for warmly welcoming us back—in spite of the tourist traffic we inevitably brought with us.*

MICHAEL PATRICK KING *For a single person, the trifecta of terror is Christmas, New Year's Eve, and Valentine's Day, because the pressure is so high. The New Year's montage was originally a Christmas Eve montage, with Carrie feeling sorry for herself. But I changed it so that the scene is more about Carrie rescuing Miranda. She is able to shift from feeling sorry for herself to doing something for someone else.*

DAVID EIGENBERG *We shot my New Year's Eve scene on a very hot day. It's supposed to be winter, but it was so hot that I was covered in sweat the entire time. We had no air conditioning, and I remember saying, "Does anyone care that I'm covered in sweat and we're supposed to be wearing mittens, gloves, and hats?"*

A call from Miranda woke Carrie. Miranda sounded choked up, and although she told Carrie to go back to sleep, Carrie offered to catch a cab and meet her. But there wasn't a taxi in sight.

SARAH JESSICA PARKER *To me, my New Year's Eve outfit is quintessential Patricia Field. I'm wearing a vintage Halston sparkly sequined hat and a vintage pajama pant with a vintage fur coat on top that I wore on the show. I loved pulling that old coat out—I reached into the pocket and there were cigarettes in it from when we wrapped in Season Five and Carrie still smoked! My shoes are very expensive white kid leather boots with black trim. When you mix vintage pieces with a nice shoe, that's when girls think, I can do that.*

CRAIG BLANKENHORN, STILL PHOTOGRAPHER *I love to photograph Sarah Jessica running in Manolo Blahniks. Any time you can get her running in shoes, it's great. She runs though the snow in this scene, from her apartment to Miranda's, and she never slips. In fact, I've never seen her fall down—on ice, snow, or steps.*

So Carrie took the subway—and reached Miranda just in time.

"You're not
alone."
CARRIE

When the girls reunited for Fashion Week, Samantha confessed that she wasn't cut out for the one-on-one relationship thing. Once they'd settled into their amazing front-row seats, Charlotte urged Miranda to forgive Steve—but admitted that she would

MICHAEL PATRICK KING *I had a minor freak-out when I saw the dress that the wardrobe department chose for Carrie's Fashion Week outfit. I had originally conceived of her as more subdued at this point in the story because of her sadness over Big. Molly Rogers had the nerve to say to me, "It's been months! We're over it—we want to see feathers!"*

MOLLY ROGERS *The Vivienne Westwood clothes in the fashion show are a mix of different seasons. Patricia picked twelve looks to come down the runway. Some of the clothes are from Westwood's archive, and some are from her spring 2008 collection.*

never forgive Big if she were Carrie. If she ever ran into him, Charlotte told the girls, she'd know exactly what to say. Carrie put Big out of her mind and, as one fabulous outfit after another came down the runway, realized she was actually enjoying herself.

PATRICIA FIELD *There was a big debate about who should be sitting in the front row for the fashion show. We all had our favorites. Fern Mallis, the president of the Council of Fashion Designers of America, is there, as well as Kelis and Lil' Kim.*

MICHAEL PATRICK KING *Initially in the fashion scene, Carrie and the girls see a model wearing Carrie's wedding dress. But when I saw Carrie get jilted on the street, I realized how goddamn painful it was, and I really didn't think the audience needed to go through another humiliation involving the dress. The fact that Carrie later finds it in her closet with Louise felt more organic. Now the fashion show is about the colors acting like smelling salts and bringing her back to life.*

On Valentine's Day, over dinner with Miranda, Carrie worried aloud that she had caused Big to leave her at the altar. Miranda finally confessed what she'd said to Big the night of the engagement party, and Carrie—furious—stormed out of the restaurant.

"I think what hurts the most is that you kept a secret from me. I have never, ever kept a secret from you. Ever!"

CARRIE

ERIC CYPHERS *The art department blew up hundreds of balloons, and tied hundreds more strings to a mesh web on the ceiling. Walking around the set with the strings rubbing on your face was like water torture.*

Meanwhile, in L.A., Samantha couldn't contain her anger when Smith came home three hours late and missed her surprise sushi dinner.

"I am not the type of woman who sits home all day waiting for a man!"
SAMANTHA

MICHAEL PATRICK KING *In an earlier version of this scene, we didn't see the sushi, but there's a saying: "Off stage is no stage." Samantha really has to put herself out there and be stood up to justify throwing the sushi. She's in this giant beach house on a table covered in sushi, with her little dog looking up at her, and she tells him, "This is bullshit!" She's gone from being the toast of the town to cold sushi on a table, talking to a dog.*

Three days after their fight, Carrie still couldn't forgive Miranda. So the two had a heart-to-heart. Carrie told Miranda it wasn't fair that Miranda expected to be forgiven so soon, yet she wouldn't forgive Steve. So Miranda decided to give couples therapy a try.

"You badger me to forgive you in three days— and you won't even consider forgiving Steve for something he did six months ago."

CARRIE

"How do I know she won't punish me for the rest of my life?"

STEVE

Later, on a walk in Central Park, Miranda told Carrie that she and Steve had made a plan: If they decided they wanted to be together again, they would both show up at an agreed-upon time on the Brooklyn Bridge—and put the past behind them.

"Poetic—if we both show up.
Otherwise, you're on a bridge,
rejected.
Not a good plan."

MIRANDA

JOHN MELFI *To shoot in Central Park, you have to cooperate with the conservancy department so you don't interfere with the trees or damage any of the landscaping. We needed special permission to bring in forsythia, since it was supposed to be spring. We were able to shoot in the Ladies' Pavilion, which had never been used in a movie before.*

Over coffee with Carrie, Louise had two pieces of good news to share. First, the apartment on Fifth Avenue had finally sold, and second, Louise was moving back to St. Louis to marry her ex, Will—and she had a diamond ring to prove it.

"This ain't rented."

LOUISE

JENNIFER HUDSON
IMPROVISED THIS LINE

JENNIFER HUDSON *It was strange to go from* Dreamgirls, *where everything was filmed in studios, to shooting outside in front of all these people. One day, while filming, I came out of the subway and people kept stopping me in the middle of the scene, saying, "Oh, my God, Jennifer Hudson!" I said, "What do I do?" Jennifer would stop and talk to everyone, but Louise couldn't.*

In L.A., Samantha—despite seeming to have it all—couldn't help but feel that something was missing from her life. When her sexy neighbor propositioned her, she found it difficult to resist the temptation and began to overeat to deal with her sexual frustration.

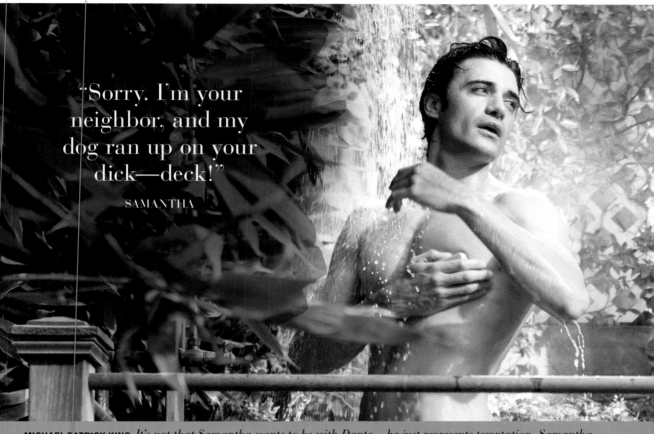

"Sorry. I'm your neighbor, and my dog ran up on your dick—deck!"

SAMANTHA

MICHAEL PATRICK KING *It's not that Samantha wants to be with Dante—he just represents temptation. Samantha sees him having sex with a different woman every night and tells Carrie, "One of the hard things about being in L.A. is my neighbor. I can't stop thinking about him. Sex with a different partner every night—he's like me five years ago." She doesn't want to have sex with him. She wants to be him.*

On the day she was supposed to meet Steve on the Brooklyn Bridge, Miranda sipped coffee in a Lower East Side café and listed the pros and cons of getting back together with him. Just as she stood to leave, she noticed some foam on her lip . . .

JOHN MELFI *The Brooklyn Bridge shoot actually went well, but you can't drive up there, so all of our equipment had to be carted up and down. We also had to work around all of the pedestrians, since you can't shut down the Brooklyn Bridge. But we were given a hundred feet of space so we could use our own extras, who wouldn't look directly into the camera.*

. . . and knew just what to do. As she arrived on the bridge, the crowd parted, and Steve appeared. Together, they headed back to Brooklyn—and never looked back.

"Kiss me."

MIRANDA

MICHAEL PATRICK KING *The last scene between Miranda and Steve, after they return home from the Brooklyn Bridge, is the most sexual scene they've ever had. To me, it is the answer to the story line: They forgot, and then they refound.*

THESE CURTAINS
WERE MADE FROM
FABRICS FOUND AT
MOOD FABRICS

THIS HEADBOARD
WAS SPECIALLY
DESIGNED FOR
THE MOVIE
AND WAS MADE
BY MARTIN
ALBERT INTERIORS

THESE BED LINENS ARE
FROM ANICHINI AND
ABC CARPET & HOME

THIS "STERN" BENCH IS
FROM LOBEL MODERN

THIS CHAIR IS FROM
AERO STUDIOS

THIS CHAIR (THE SAME AS
THE ONE AT CARRIE'S DESK)
IS FROM MODERN LIVING
SUPPLIES AND WAS DESIGNED
BY TOMMI PARZINGER

THIS "OVERLEAF" RUG IS
FROM THE RUG COMPANY AND
WAS DESIGNED BY MARNI

THIS MIRRORED VANITY
IS FROM ALAN MOSS

CARRIE DOESN'T LOVE HERE ANYMORE

There are many ways in which *Sex and the City: The Movie* is an atypical romantic comedy, but one of the more intriguing is that there are two makeovers in the film. Carrie gets a makeover when she colors her hair, and her apartment gets a makeover when she decides to try to get over Big and get her life in order.

For much of the movie, however, Carrie's apartment looks exactly as it did on the series, and reassembling it after nearly four years turned out to be an enormous challenge. When the show wrapped, production designer Jeremy Conway had his staff save all of the drawings, paint samples, and wallpaper in case there was a movie. "We put together about twenty boxes of all of our drawings and the swing sets. There was a binder that showed exactly what was in all of the boxes, and we gave everything to HBO. When we finally got around to making the film, though, it turned out that the boxes were nowhere to be found."

Fortunately, Conway and his crew were able to bring the room to life. A painter would remember a color, an art director would supply drawings of Carrie's apartment, and gradually the sets came together.

Sarah Jessica Parker was also tremendously helpful in tracking down some of the furniture. She had taken key pieces and stored them, and associate producer Melinda Relyea had archived everything with photographs. Some pieces had been sold; others had been auctioned off for charity (like the Aidan chair, which Parker donated to a giant tag sale benefiting New York City public schools); and Carrie's desk, chair, and computer had been given to the Smithsonian Institution.

It was these last three items that proved to be the most difficult to retrieve. Initially, the Smithsonian said no. "I was on the phone with this gentleman at the museum," remembers Parker, "and he said, 'It's understood that when you give us something, it's a deed for life.' But I am a very superstitious person, so I said, 'I understand that, but we can't reproduce the desk. It will never be the same.'

I told him we would do whatever was needed to return everything to them safely. He said, 'Will you sign a deed for life after this?' and I said yes. He gave us everything except the computer, which was actually fine because computers get outdated pretty quickly. I thought Carrie would have upgraded by now."

When it came time to give such an iconic set a makeover, Conway was adamant that it be done right, in a way that was true to Carrie, even if it was completely different from her old apartment. "Michael Patrick King had told me that when Carrie redecorates, she makes her apartment more grown-up," Conway recalls. "I asked him, 'How grown-up is it? Is she putting a lot of money into it? Is there a decorator involved?' The apartment reflects where she's headed with her life: It's more sophisticated and not as cluttered."

The biggest difference is in the kitchen, although Conway acknowledges, as would befit takeout queen Carrie, "It's probably never used." As for the rest,

it still has Carrie's touch in that it's bold—in deep blues and off-whites—and has a sense of humor.

"Over her bed there are lots of framed photos and mementos on the wall," says Conway. "We also added a little dining area where the big, long bookshelves used to be, because we thought Carrie would want a place where she could serve dinner instead of making people sit around the coffee table in her living room. All of her books and magazines went into a unit that is now in the living room. It has glossy doors that we painted with scripted quotes from Gertrude Stein."

And what did Parker think of the makeover? "I don't know that it's my own taste," she admits, "but I think it photographs really well. There are things about it that I love and others that make me think, She hired a decorator to do that. But ultimately it's right for Carrie, and it's so much cleaner. If you're emotionally cleaning out your life, this is what you do."

At her newly redecorated apartment, a back-to-blonde Carrie got ready to throw a party. When Samantha arrived, she rendered the girls speechless with her two new "pooches"—the one in her bag and the one around her middle.

"Did you ever think you'd see the day— me with a pooch?"
SAMANTHA

KIM CATTRALL *For the pooch scene, Patricia Field put me in these pants that were too tight at the waist, and the top was too tight on my arms, which made them look bigger. With the shooting schedule the way it was, I couldn't pull a Robert De Niro and actually gain weight.*

Samantha explained that she had to eat so she wouldn't cheat, and when the girls asked if she was happy, she admitted she hadn't felt truly happy in six months.

"What does your gut tell you?"

CARRIE

JOHN MELFI *We had to use a body double for this scene, and Kim slouched a little to make it look believable. It was a challenge to find a double who would work with Kim's body.*

Back in L.A., Samantha admitted her true feelings and broke up with Smith, assuring him he would find a woman who wanted a long-term relationship. She considered returning the petal ring, but in the end decided to keep it—as a reminder of him.

"I love you, but I love me more. I've been in a relationship with myself for forty-nine years, and that's the one I need to work on."

SAMANTHA

MICHAEL PATRICK KING *Samantha had everything—the most gorgeous man, a $4 million beach house—but it's not enough. I wanted her to end up single at the end of the movie. It's a brave move—she chooses a life that's about her versus what everyone says she should have. That's the moral for Samantha: It doesn't matter how old you are or what trappings of society you have. If you're not being true to yourself, you're never going to be happy.*

Samantha returned to New York—and moved into Miranda's apartment on the Lower East Side. Meanwhile, Carrie said a tearful good-bye to Louise and thanked her for bringing her back to life.

KIM CATTRALL *The thing that I love about the movie is that Samantha's the only one who is single at the end. At the end of the series, Carrie was the only one who was single—she was with Big, but it was ambiguous how long their relationship would last.*

On the Upper East Side, a very pregnant Charlotte panicked when she spotted Big having lunch alone. She tried to sneak away unnoticed, but he saw her and followed her outside, where Charlotte blurted out the words she'd been saving up for him.

MICHAEL PATRICK KING *The very first time we were shooting the scene where Charlotte's water breaks, the Catholic girls' school across the street had a fire drill. All of a sudden, the school doors opened and these teenage girls came out in long plaid uniform skirts. When they saw Chris Noth, they came running across the street, screaming, "I love you!" He said, "Aren't you supposed to be in school?" And they said, "Absofuckinglutely!"*

But before Charlotte could escape in a taxi, her water broke, and Big insisted on rushing her to the hospital in his car.

"I curse the day you were born!"

CHARLOTTE

KRISTIN DAVIS *This was a hard scene. It was my first day on the set, so I had to work backward emotionally. But Chris Noth tried really hard to be serious—which is an effort for him! I had often felt, during the series, that Charlotte should have been allowed to show more anger, so I thought it was great that she would let Big have it after what he had done to Carrie.*

At the hospital, Carrie congratulated Charlotte and Harry on the birth of their beautiful baby daughter, whom they named Rose. But Carrie was thrown when Charlotte told her Big had waited at the hospital hoping to see her.

THIS SCENE WAS FILMED AT LENOX HILL HOSPITAL, ON MANHATTAN'S UPPER EAST SIDE

KRISTIN DAVIS *I love Charlotte's ending. It is beautiful, and because of everything she has been through, it doesn't seem like a fairy tale. She learned a lot of lessons on the series and loosened up a lot of her "rules," and that's why I think she eventually gets everything she wanted. I feel so satisfied to have gotten to follow her story through to its conclusion.*

Harry told Carrie that Big had been writing to her—but Carrie insisted that she had never received any letters.

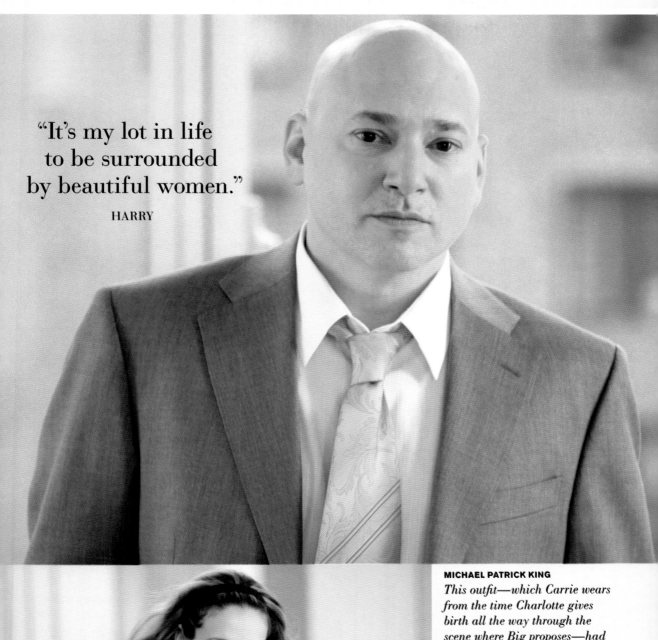

"It's my lot in life
to be surrounded
by beautiful women."

HARRY

MICHAEL PATRICK KING
This outfit—which Carrie wears from the time Charlotte gives birth all the way through the scene where Big proposes—had to be something that you wouldn't get tired of seeing, but it also had to be something she would believably wear when writing. The wardrobe department came up with this pale green Nina Ricci slip dress and paired it with the Dior Extreme shoes. Then they made the jacket, which is a vintage Givenchy jacket that they deconstructed and combined with a leather Members Only motorcycle jacket. It's a perfect example of the craft and thought that the wardrobe department put into everything.

Carrie rushed home and checked her mail—but found nothing from Big. Remembering that Louise created a special e-mail file to hide his messages, she called her to ask where to find them.

Inside the file, Carrie found one very special love letter. So she rushed to the Fifth Avenue apartment in a taxi—hoping to catch Big before it was too late.

"I know
I screwed it up—
but I will love you
forever."

BIG

Carrie walked into what looked like an empty apartment and made her way to the closet—where she found Big, alone, holding her Manolos. She threw her arms around him, and they kissed. It wasn't logic—it was love.

Afterward, they admitted they had both been perfectly happy before they decided to "live happily ever after." Suddenly, Big was down on one knee asking Carrie to marry him—and slipping Carrie's Manolo on her foot, Cinderella-style.

SARAH JESSICA PARKER *It took a long time to shoot this scene with Chris. You're in a closet, and all of a sudden you realize the camera can only do certain things. And the problem with Chris is that he starts laughing, and then I started laughing, and suddenly it's four in the morning. It's so unprofessional, yet funny.*

"Carrie Bradshaw, love of my life, will you marry me?"

Big and Carrie finally married at City Hall, with Carrie in her label-less suit—just as they had originally planned.

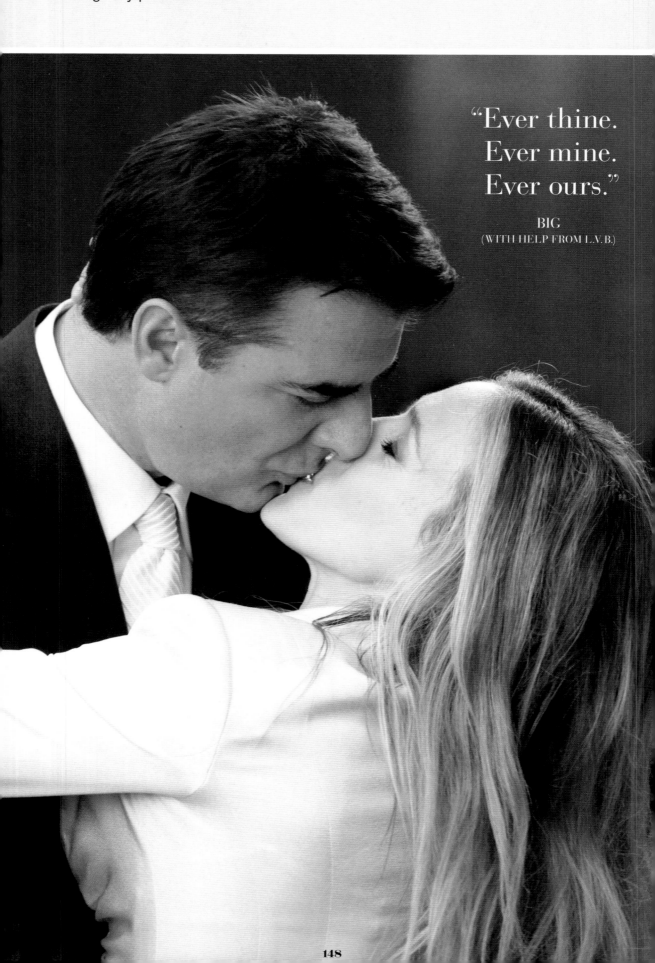

"Ever thine.
Ever mine.
Ever ours."

BIG
(WITH HELP FROM L.V.B.)

After the ceremony, Carrie was surprised to find Miranda, Charlotte, and Samantha waiting outside the courtroom. Big had invited them, knowing his bride would want to share the day with her closest friends.

SARAH JESSICA PARKER *When we started thinking about the right shoe for Carrie's wedding, I asked Michael Patrick, "Is it about a Manolo? Because that might not happen today. It's nice for nostalgic reasons, but since the show went off the air, there have been a lot of other designers who have done some exciting things." He said he just wanted it to be the perfect shoe. We talked to the people at Manolo about our ideas, and they produced all these incredible shoes. They did two colors of blue—one lighter and one this true electric blue with a pewter buckle on it covered in rhinestones. It was just perfect. Also, I begged Jeremy Conway, our production designer, to place the official seal of New York on this floor, so he and his team created it. It was so magnificent.*

MICHAEL PATRICK KING *Initially, Carrie was going to come outside of City Hall and the girls were going to be waiting for her, but we moved the scene inside so as not to risk giving away the ending. Instead, the girls are waiting for Carrie on the other side of the door. The day we shot, Sarah Jessica wore a big coat to hide the vintage suit.*

The girls and Big were joined by Steve, Brady, Harry, Lily, Rose, Stanford, and Anthony for a low-key reception at Junior's diner. Big ordered ham and eggs, exactly as he had wanted it.

KIM CATTRALL *The last scene I had with the whole cast was at Junior's after Big and Carrie's wedding. I looked around the table, and here were these people with whom I've spent the last ten years of my life. Some of them were babies when I first met them—like the boy who plays Cynthia's son on the show—so I really got emotional. Sex and the City has been a seminal part of our lives, and the movie gave us this amazing opportunity to be together again. It's the biggest dysfunctional family you could ever want to belong to.*

SARAH JESSICA PARKER *I think in many ways this was one of the funniest days on the shoot—in large part because all of us, Willie Garson and Mario Cantone included, were together. It's the only scene that allowed for that. And, truly, it was as if we had been kept apart from each other for years. We couldn't stop laughing and couldn't stop eating, and I think Michael Patrick reconciled that he had little or no control, so he let Joe Collins and Mike O'Shea just start rolling the cameras and get everything on film. In my opinion, that day ended far too early. I could have stayed there with that group for many, many more hours.*

Later, with the help of a new pair of glasses, Carrie gave a reading from her latest book. After everything she'd been through, she was finally able to see what she should have known all along: that everything she'd ever wanted was right there in front of her.

MICHAEL PATRICK KING *On the surface, the glasses Carrie finally wears in this scene are a funny commentary on getting older—and not accepting it. But, on a deeper level, they also represent the idea that she can finally "see" who she is—and where she is in her life.*

SEX AND THE CITY (Book 1)

ADVANCE PRAISE FOR

SEX AND THE CITY AND
Carrie Bradshaw

"Surprising and shocking. . . . A completely odd compilation . . . showing the wit of the early Whitman . . . . Very strange and often brilliant, this is an insider's view of lifestyles in the city—within the city that never sleeps, for good reason and ever better instinct, despite the fact that love thrives as if it never existed"—Reviews-r-us.com

"Dramatic, powerfully clear and keenly reported . . . Bradshaw provides direct and breathtaking insights in a loveless hue. . . . The result is too much of a good thing—like pudding tinged with more than a dollop of sour cream . . . This writing is comfort food for the brain stem, and will appeal to anyone fitted with such." —Books Bi-Weekly

"Compelling, stabbing, biting and blessedly written. You should be teased by anyone this clever and experienced, . . . prior to the recognition that Carrie Bradshaw has stolen your heart. (The fact that you may have lost a kidney laughing at the same time is stunning literary achievement in and of itself.) People that don't love this book are beyond help and immune to the songs of the snake charmer. They will be spending time looking over shoulder lest Bradshaw spy them" —Eric Viagi Putard

In racking up the score, she lives the life that many of us dream and never risk. Late night misadventures, courtesy of powerful primal biological urges, are grist for the pepper shaker—and when the waiter tells you his name it is Bradshaw that reports back. Even as she searches the late night haunts of the 'culture-vulture-ati,' the blistering trail of collateral damage evoked by tweaked super-egos and frisky hands is faithfully observed, and between short breaths, memorialized in a contract of language that lives beyond the edge of prudent thinking.

Sex and the City is a chronicle of the 'Circus Maximus' that is captivated by the heart and mind of the modern urban dweller. While tribe-like groups of lovelorn avengers cluster in bars, at parties and outside clubs hunting for a mate, Bradshaw provides the when, where and how to go home with a stranger. Warning!... You are about to enter a world that is quaking with anticipation, shaking with pleasure, and pounding to the beat of a very different (and sexy) drummer.

An acclaimed writer, Carrie Bradshaw writes the "Sex and the City" column in the New York Star. She is also a regular contributor to Vogue. Ms. Bradshaw lives in New York City.

ISBN 0-394-58443-0

SEX AND THE CITY

$21

Savvy, cutting and rigorous, Carrie Bradshaw's 'Sex and the City,' column in Vogue and the New York Star has attracted critical acclaim, seating her squarely on a super-starved thrown. This compilation puts her bits of wisdom where they can be read in the discomfort of modern existential angst, while longing for a true passionate experience.

This is strange narrative, turning a light on a style of horizontal Mambo that only the culturally gifted enjoy. 'Sex and the City' makes theater of the many galas and distractions that "New York players" find essential to status hikes. Not lacking insight, Ms. Bradshaw's pithy writing places you among the men who score models, "Modelizers," teaches about the hand signals of the aptly named "Jerk Off Johns" and "Needy Neanderthals" who drive the best of us crazy, while providing a piercing witnessing of a gaggle of romances with our Carrie, perturbed author with "Mr. Big," mega-schmutz, "Samantha Jones," the publicist with sundry dudes, the career challenged, "Mumsford Blanche," and the skivy prop master, "Skimpy Peanut" and with the women of "Just Say No." It is a proven fact that Carrie comes home late with tales that scream to be told, but are best whispered to the nearest consenting adult.

Clearwater Press

Carrie Bradshaw

A SINGLE LIFE (Book 2)

A SINGLE LIFE
CARRIE BRADSHAW

PRAISE FOR CARRIE BRADSHAW AND

A SINGLE LIFE

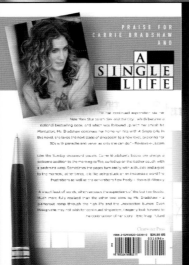

Clearwater Press

A SINGLE LIFE

PRAISE FOR CARRIE BRADSHAW

New York City's Bestseller Author On Single Life In the Big City

CARRIE BRADSHAW

MENHATTAN (Book 3)

CARRIE BRADSHAW

MENHATTAN

MENHATTAN

PRAISE FOR CARRIE BRADSHAW

"To define New York City, and the men who reside on our island takes just one voice - Carrie Bradshaw. Her poignant observations towards dating and the mindset of the single man in the city continues to be spot-on in searing accuracy. It will leave you in tears of laughter and touching honesty. A cornucopia of experiences" -Books Bi-Weekly

"Witty, concise, with ascerbic focus on the XY gender anomaly that resides in America's city island. A strong continuation on the notable findings of Ms. Bradshaw. Sin for the intellectual senses, with a dollop of sarcastic nirvana." -Reviews-r-us.com

"A sultry walk on a crisp fall day through Central Park with Ms. Bradshaw, spotting the dearth of manhood - and lack thereof - in the most acute writing. She stole my heart before, and now I am just a puddle on the wet sidewalk of her writer's stoop. May her keen observations continue indefinitely" - Eric Viagi Putard

MENHATTAN

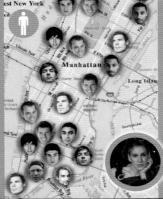

PRAISE FOR CARRIE BRADSHAW

Another Inspired Look at Single Life in The Big City by Bestselling Author
CARRIE BRADSHAW

MICHAEL PATRICK KING *At the bookstore, Carrie reads from her book in progress and says, "As I put my wedding gown away, I couldn't help but wonder, Why are we all so willing to write our own vows—but not our own rules?" Big and Carrie were perfectly fine until they thought, Maybe we should change something. You get into trouble when you decide to live happily ever after. The series is about choosing your own path over society's path. In this particular confection, it's about Carrie getting hoodwinked by society's idea of being a bride and Big losing sight*

And there, in the city where they met as girls, four New York women entered the next phase of their lives . . . dressed head to toe in love.

MICHAEL PATRICK KING *We wanted the club in the final scene to be like Brigadoon—not any place that actually exists. So we filmed the exterior at the Vitra furniture store on Ninth Avenue, next to SoHo House, and the interior at designer Diane von Furstenberg's studio on 14th and Washington Streets. I wanted the four girls to go down into a club so we could have the shot of the twentysomething girls running up the street as the camera floats away. Only the twentysomething girls were waiting in line, trying to get in. Carrie Bradshaw will always be on the list.*

SARAH JESSICA PARKER *This scene reminded me of the beginning of the show. The way the four women are laughing and navigating the cobblestone streets in ridiculously high heels, backlit by the night sky, and New York City, and the joy of being with one another—that's how it all started. Sometimes, when we were shooting certain scenes, it was as if time stood still. All else faded away and it was just these four women—yes, older, and hopefully somewhat wiser, but still completely devoted to their dreams, their city, and each other. I loved having this be the last shot of our movie. This is exactly how it should have ended.*

. . . and they lived
fabulously ever after.

THE LOOK BOOK
WHAT THEY WORE FROM HEAD TO TOE

When you think *Sex and the City*, you think of the sex and the city, of course, but you also think of the clothes. Patricia Field and Molly Rogers have been the show's costume designers since Season One, helping to define its signature style: over-the-top, colorful, and a mash-up of couture and street. When Field and Rogers were hired to design costumes for the movie, they assembled a team that consisted of old and new, adding Paolo Nieddu and Danny Santiago. "We needed a mix of great stylists and great shoppers," says Field. "Paolo had worked in my store and had started styling Scarlett Johansson. He was young and excited, with good taste and energy. And Danny is the best stylist in Miami. He does a lot of covers for *W* magazine. He has a refined sense of taste and owns a vintage warehouse."

In conceiving the wardrobes for the movie, Field and Rogers knew that they would have to raise the already-high bar that had been set by the show. "Pat got everything she wanted for Christmas," says writer and director Michael Patrick King. "The clothes are phenomenal—even bigger than they were in the series." Indeed, the clothing in the movie is by some of the best-known designer names in the business: Sonia Rykiel, Salvatore Ferragamo, Chanel, Christian Dior, Dolce & Gabbana, Ralph Lauren, Nina Ricci, Donna Karan, Yves Saint Laurent, Alexander McQueen, and, of course, Vivienne Westwood. "Pat had a vision of how the characters' lives had evolved," says King. "Her instincts were impeccable and beyond reproach."

But is it realistic that the characters' wardrobe budgets would have expanded to the level they did? "Every character is a little more stylish in the movie than she was in the series," says King. "As a writer, initially I wasn't sure how realistic it was to have Miranda dressing the way she does, for example, but then I think about Carrie bringing that *mille feuille* dress to Paris in the finale. You had to wonder how she got it in her suitcase, but it turned out to be a defining moment of the series. Sometimes fashion trumps logic. So for the film, I decided to just go for it. The girls are still grounded."

Assembling pieces from couture houses proved to be a challenge—especially with pre-production going on in August, when everyone in Europe is on vacation. Favors were called in, connections worked,

and pieces were borrowed, little by little. There were approximately 320 costumes for the four leading women, plus jewelry, shoes, and bags. Charlotte, Miranda, and Samantha wear about forty outfits each, while Carrie wears about eighty.

"The wardrobe department had to do an enormous amount of work," says producer John Melfi, "and then they had the additional cast members to dress, as well as all of the background players. So hundreds of costumes had to be prepped in eight weeks, with the cooperation of every fashion house in New York, Paris, London, and Rome. It was amazing that so many of them cooperated."

Because many of the higher-end pieces were borrowed, they had to be returned immediately after they were worn—sometimes within minutes. "It was very hard to coordinate the wardrobe," says Sarah Jessica Parker, "because the fashion shows were going on in Milan and Paris. On the rare occasion when someone was willing to loan us something, we would only have it for a few hours and then someone would have to take it back."

As any moviegoer can see, the costumes in the movie have an extravagant, cotton-candy quality, but during Carrie's dark period—which takes up almost an hour of the film—her clothes are toned down. "We filmed all the big statement scenes early because they all took place on the streets," explains King. "We wanted to give people the impression that the costumes were going to be huge. But what I like about the movie is that the tone fluctuates: One minute it's calm, then it's gigantic, and then it's calm again. For every scene in which Miranda is in an amazing gown, there's another where she's wearing an old T-shirt."

Ultimately, Field and Rogers wanted the clothes to reflect what had happened to the characters in the four years since the audience last saw them. "Everything you do you need to do for a reason. It can't be chaos," says Field. "So when it came to the movie, I asked myself, What are we going to do for our seventh act? I knew the looks had to be heightened, but at the same time the girls couldn't change from black to white, because the audience knows them too intimately. In the end, we changed them just enough to take the movie in a new, but still familiar, direction."

DRESS: *Vintage*
SHOES: *Dior Extreme*
CLUTCH: *Castor & Pollux*

SWEATER: *Prada*
BRA: *H&M*
PANTIES: *Calvin Klein*
SHOES: *Walter Steiger*

DRESS: *L.A.M.B.*
SHOES: *Manolo Blah*
BAG: *Salvatore Ferrag*

DRESS: *Vena Cava*
NECKLACE:
Carol Tannenbaum

DRESS: *Vintage*
BELT: *Vintage*
SHOES: *Dior*
BAG: *Chanel*

DRESS: *Nieves Lavi*
TOP: *Giorgio Armani* SWEATER: *Tomas Maier*
SHOES: *Valentino* BAG: *Prada*

DRESS: *Yves Saint Laurent*
SHOES: *Nina Ricci*

TOP: *Rick Owens*
PANTS: *Bitten* BAG: *Hermès*
SHOES: *Christian Louboutin*

TOP: *The Lake & Sta*
JEANS: *Totem*

SUIT: *Ralph Lauren*
SHOES: *Manolo Blahnik*
CLUTCH: *Judith Leiber*
BROOCH: *Verdura*

PONCHO: *Nina Ricci*

ROBE: *Vintage*
Norma Kamali

COAT & DRESS: *Vintage*
BELT: *Vintage*
BAG: *Timmy Woods*
BRACELET: *Verdura*

DRESS: *Vintage*
SHOES: *Manolo Blahnik*
CLUTCH: *Fendi*
EARRINGS: *Fred Leighton*

DRESS: *Missoni*

DRESS: *YaYa*
CLUTCH: *Vintage*
BRACELET: *Jennifer Fisher*

VEST: *Proenza Schouler*
SKIRT: *Vintage*
SHOES: *Proenza Schouler*
BAG: *Kisim*

DRESS: *Vivienne Westwood*
BELT: *Vintage*
SHOES: *Manolo Blahnik*
BAG: *Salvatore Ferragamo*

JACKET: *L'Wren Scott*
DRESS: *John Galliano*
BELT: *Vintage*

DRESS: *Calvin Klein*
SHOES: *Giuseppe Zanotti*

DRESS: *Zac Posen*
SHOES: *Christian Louboutin*
BAG: *Yves Saint Laurent*

DRESS: *YaYa*

DRESS:
Veronique Branquinho

JUMPSUIT: *Sonia Rykiel*
SHOES: *Christian Louboutin*
BELT: *Vintage* CLUTCH: *VBH*

ROBE: *Agent Provocateur*
SHOES: *Agent Provocateur*

DRESS: *Vivienne Westwood*

COAT: *Dior*
LEGGINGS: *Splendid*
SHOES: *Dior Extreme*
FUR: *J. Mendel*

ROBE: *Vintage*

COVER-UP: *Vintage*
BATHING SUIT: *Lucien*
SUNGLASSES: *Oliver Peoples*

DRESS: *Alexander McQueen*
SHOES: *Matt Bernson*
NECKLACES: *Fred Leighton*

TOP: *Splendid*
HAT: *Hermès*

COAT: *Burberry*
PANTS: *Balenciaga*
HAT: *Miu Miu*

TEE: *Daft Bird*
TOP: *Vince*
PANTS: *L'Wren Scott*

COAT: *Rick Owens*
DRESS: *Kristensen du Nord*
SHOES: *Sergio Rossi*

COAT: *Vintage*

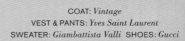

COAT: *Vionnet*
SCARF: *Valentino*
SHOES: *Azzedine Alaïa*

COAT: *Proenza Schouler*
TEE: *Katharine Hamnett*
DRESS: *Frankie Morello*

DRESS: *Emma Domb*
SHOES: *Manolo Blahnik*
NECKLACES: *Vintage*

COAT: *Vintage*
VEST & PANTS: *Yves Saint Laurent*
SWEATER: *Giambattista Valli* SHOES: *Gucci*

DRESS: *Moose Kinsey*
SHOES: *Charles Jourdan*
NECKLACE: *Masha Archer*

JACKET: *Vintage*
PANTS: *Margiela*
SHOES: *Chanel*
SCARF: *Chanel*

SWEATER: *Proenza Schouler*
NECKLACE: *Black Diamonds by Itay Malkin*

TOP: *New Legends*
PANTS: *Rachel Mara*
SHOES: *Roger Vivier*

TOP: *Chanel*
CATSUIT: *B with G*
NECKLACE: *Mikomoto*

COAT: *Vintage*
SHOES: *Sigerson Morrison*
HAT: *Vintage Halston*
BAG: *VBH*

DRESS: *Dolce & Gabbana*
FUR: *Lucien Pellat-Finet*
SHOES: *Sigerson Morrison*
BAG: *Vintage*

COAT & DRESS: *Alexander Wang*
SHOES: *Dior Extreme*
SCARF: *Chanel*

SWEATER: *Demylee*
JEANS: *Totem*

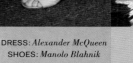

SS: *Alexander dell'Acqua*
SHOES: *Nina Ricci*
EARRINGS: *Jennifer Fisher*

DRESS: *Nina Ricci*
SHOES: *Dior Extreme*
BAG: *Louis Vuitton*

JACKET: *Vintage*   SKIRT: *Vintage*
SHOES: *Manolo Blahnik*
CLUTCH: *Barbara Bolan*

DRESS: *Alexander McQueen*
SHOES: *Manolo Blahnik*

DRESS: *Vintage Yves Saint Laurent*
SHOES: *Dior Extreme*

CHARLOTTE

Jackie O. Meets
Upper East Side Mommy

DRESS & SHOES: *Prada*
BAG: *Chanel*
SUNGLASSES: *Salt Optical*

DRESS: *Issa*
BRACELET: *Chanel*

TOP: *Ter et Bantine*
BRACELET: *Lia Sophia*

DRESS: *Vintage*
SHOES: *Phillipe and
David Blonde*
BAG: *Chanel*

DRESS: *Tibi*

DRESS: *Oscar de la Ren...*
SHOES: *Gianmarco Lore...*
EARRINGS: *Kenneth Jay I...*

DRESS: *Salvatore Ferragamo*
BELT: *Vintage* SHOES: *Christian Louboutin*
EARRINGS: *H. Stern*

COAT: *Peter Som*
TOP: *Prada*
PANTS: *A Pea in the Pod*

VEST: *A Pea in the Pod*
TOP: *Nike* PANTS: *Fila*
EARMUFFS: *Chanel*

DRESS: *Azzaro*
NECKLACE: *H. Stern*

DRESS: *Prada*
NECKLACE: *Jennifer Fisher*

TOP: *Valentino*
SKIRT: *Prada*
BRACELET: *H. Stern*

DRESS: *Valentino*

TOP: *Miu Miu*

DRESS: *Oscar de la Renta*
NECKLACE: *Cartier*

DRESS: *Zac Posen*
BAG: *Chanel*

BATHING SUIT: *Eres*
SHOES: *Giuseppe Zanotti*

DRESS: *Antonio Berardi*
TOP: *Tuleh*

DRESS: *Jil Sander*
JACKET: *Valentino*
CLUTCH: *Chanel*

DRESS: *James Perse*

RESS: *Gianfranco Ferré*
ES: *Prada* TOP: *Valentino*
OCH: *Chanel* BAG: *Fendi*

DRESS: *Oscar de la Renta*
SHOES: *Dior*
EARRINGS: *H. Stern*

COAT: *Prada*
DRESS: *Oscar de la Renta*

PAJAMAS: *Brooks Brothers*

DRESS & BELT: *Chanel*
JACKET: *6267*
BAG: *Nancy Gonzalez*

DRESS: *Vicki Teal*
SHOES: *Miu Miu*
NECKLACE: *H. Stern*

MIRANDA

Brooklyn Mom Meets Power Lawyer

DRESS: *Alberta Ferretti*
BELT: *Carlos Falchi*
SHOES: *Luciano Padovan*
BAG: *Nancy Gonzalez*

DRESS: *Maggie London*
BELT: *Vintage*
SHOES: *Gucci*
BAG: *Alexander McQueen*

DRESS: *Ports 1961*
EARRINGS: *Lia Sophia*

DRESS: *Vintage*
EARRINGS: *Bismark*

DRESS: *Zac Posen*
CLUTCH: *Judith Leiber*

DRESS: *Vivienne Tam*
SHOES: *Casadei*
BAG: *Hollywould*

COAT: *Charlotte Ronson* DRESS: *Natalie Eshkenasy*
SHOES: *Oscar de la Renta* BAG: *Stuart Weitzman*

COAT: *J. Mendel*
DRESS: *Prada*
BAG: *Bulgari*

JACKET: *Valentino*
NECKLACE: *Versace*

JACKET: *Piazza Sempione*
DRESS: *Elie Tahari*

TOP: *BCBG*

DRESS: *Sinéquanone*
EARRINGS: *Vintage*
RING: *Yossi Harari*

DRESS: *Doucette Duvall*

DRESS: *Sonia Rykiel*
BELT: *Calvin Klein*

DRESS: *Doucette Duvall*
BELT: *Hermès*
EARRINGS: *Yossi Harari*

DRESS: *Tibi*
BELT: *Vintage*

BATHING SUIT: *Norma Kamali*
SUNGLASSES: *Calvin Klein*

DRESS: *T-Bags*
SHOES: *Casañer*

COVER-UP: *Milly*
BATHING SUIT: *Milly*

SWEATER: *Donna Karan*
PANTS: *Seven*
SHOES: *Marc Jacobs*

DRESS: *Michael Kors*
SHOES: *Roberto Cavalli*

COAT: *Bill Blass*
TOP: *Rebecca Beeson*
JEANS: *Levi's* BOOTS: *Chanel*

JACKET: *No Dress Code*
TOP: *Natalie Eshkenasy*
SHOES: *Oscar de la Renta*

DRESS: *Christian Dior*

COAT: *Valentino*
DRESS: *Peter Som*
BELT: *Kay Unger*

DRESS: *Carolina Herrera*
SHOES: *Brian Atwood*
EARRINGS: *H. Stern*

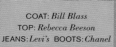

SAMANTHA

Sexy Sophisticate
Goes Malibu

JACKET: *Thierry Mugler*
SKIRT: *Valentino*
SHOES: *Roberto Cavalli*
BAG: *Fendi*

JACKET: *Thierry Mugler*
SKIRT: *Hervé Leger*
EARRINGS: *Jacob & Co.*
SUNGLASSES: *Baby Phat*

DRESS: *Zac Posen*
BRACELET: *H. Stern*
EARRINGS: *Jacob & Co.*
HAIR PIN: *Dulken & Derrick*

DRESS: *Hervé Léger*
HAT: *Sonia Rykiel*
SHOES: *Jimmy Choo*
BAG: *Rebecca Minkoff*

DRESS: *Lanvin*
EARRINGS: *Roberto Cav*

TOP: *Kenzo* SKIRT: *Zac Posen*
BELT: *Patricia Von Muslin*
SHOES: *Vicini* BAG: *Alini*

DRESS: *Versace*
SHOES: *Jimmy Choo*
BAG: *Nancy Gonzalez*

ROBE: *Chanel*
EARRINGS: *Kenneth
Jay Lane*

COAT: *Furs by PK*
CLUTCH: *Steve Madde*
GLOVES: *Sonia Rykie*

TOP: *Iceberg*
SKIRT: *Chanel*
ES: *Louis Vuitton*

TOP: *La Perla*
COVER-UP: *Pucci*

DRESS: *Halston*
BELT: *Peter Som*
NECKLACE: *Versace*
EARRINGS: *Jacob & Co.*

JACKET: *Thierry Mugler*
SKIRT: *Dior*

DRESS: *CD Greene*
EARRINGS: *Jacob & Co.*

HING SUIT: *OndadeMar*
GLASSES: *Louis Vuitton*

DRESS: *Vintage*
SHOES: *Patricia Field*
CLUTCH: *Oscar de la Renta*

BATHING SUIT: *Carmen Marc Valvo*
COVER-UP: *House of Field*
SUNGLASSES: *Louis Vuitton*

DRESS: *Halston*
EARRINGS: *Noir*

JUMPSUIT: *Vintage*
Stephen Burrows

OBE: *Jenny Packham*

TOP: *Narciso Rodriguez*

COAT: *Jenny Packham*
TOP/PANTS: *Roberto Cavalli*
BOOTS: *Jimmy Choo*

TOP: *Donna Karan*
PANTS: *Diane von Furstenberg*

COAT: *Versace*
DRESS: *Versace*

DRESS: *CD Greene*
SHOES: *Stuart Weitzman*
BAG: *Swarovski*

SEX MARKS THE SPOT
FILMING ON LOCATION

When people talk about *Sex and the City*, they tend to focus on the sex, but the city of New York is as important a character as Carrie, Miranda, Samantha, or Charlotte. Just as they did on the series, the crew shot on location in New York City as much as possible.

While the series made hot spots out of such places as the Manolo Blahnik store, Magnolia Bakery, Sushi Samba, and Payard Patisserie, the movie introduces fans to many new locations, such as the Mercer Hotel, Christie's auction house, and, most memorably, the New York Public Library. Writer and director Michael Patrick King knew that the city had to play a significant role in the movie, which is one of the reasons he chose to have Big and Carrie's wedding debacle take place at the library—a stunning

location that will transform millions of viewers into devoted NYPL fans, if only so they can walk down its beautiful staircase.

For the show, the crew often shot on the street and in lesser-known bars and restaurants, but for the movie their ambitions were much grander: Big and Carrie's engagement party takes place at Buddakan; Miranda and Steve reunite on the Brooklyn Bridge; and Carrie and Louise have drinks at Bemelmans Bar at the Carlyle hotel. Ultimately, the film evokes New York's glitz and glamour, as well as its timeless charm. A brief look at the film's locations provides a unique walking tour of interest to *Sex* devotees, movie lovers, and anyone who "hearts" the Big Apple.

202
NINTH AVENUE AT 16TH STREET

Where Miranda decides to forgive Steve

Owned by designer Nicole Farhi and located in the Chelsea Market, 202 offers a British-Mediterranean brunch menu alongside carefully chosen items from Farhi's interiors and clothing collections.

BRYANT PARK
SIXTH AVENUE AT 42ND STREET

Where the girls attend New York Fashion Week

In 1884 Reservoir Square was renamed Bryant Park to honor poet and journalist William Cullen Bryant. The park, which is located behind the main branch of the New York Public Library, offers a peaceful oasis where New Yorkers can gather to chat and relax throughout the year. It is also home to New York Fashion Week every February and September.

BUDDAKAN
NINTH AVENUE AT 16TH STREET

Where Carrie and Big host their engagement party

This 16,000-square-foot modern Asian restaurant opened in the spring of 2006 in a former Nabisco cookie factory and has been wowing New Yorkers with its stunning design and innovative cuisine ever since. Its hallmark is the Chinoiserie, a room with breathtaking chandeliers, cavernous ceilings, and a banquet table that seats thirty.

THE CARLYLE HOTEL BEMELMANS BAR
76TH STREET
BETWEEN PARK & MADISON AVENUES

Where Carrie and Louise have drinks

This high-society bar features murals of Central Park by Ludwig Bemelmans, creator of the *Madeline* children's book series, and has hosted politicians, movie stars, and other luminaries in its more-than-fifty-year history. With its art deco décor and gold leaf–covered ceiling, it is classic New York through and through.

CARRIE & BIG'S PENTHOUSE
FIFTH AVENUE AT 82ND STREET

Carrie and Big's apartment is located on New York's historic museum mile, directly across from the Metropolitan Museum of Art. The building was only used for exterior shots in the movie, while the interiors were shot in a four-story Spanish-style town house twenty blocks to the south.

CENTRAL PARK LADIES' PAVILION
CENTRAL PARK WEST
BETWEEN 75TH & 76TH STREETS

Where Carrie and Miranda talk about forgiving Steve

This charming Victorian cast-iron pavilion originally served as a shelter for people waiting for the trolley at 8th Avenue and 59th Street. It was moved to the Hernshead section of the park in 1912 and provides beautiful views of the lake.

CENTRAL PARK RESERVOIR
86TH–96TH STREETS BETWEEN CENTRAL PARK WEST & 5TH AVENUE

Where Charlotte goes jogging

Built between 1858 and 1862, the Central Park Reservoir covers one-eighth of the park's total surface. It is probably best known as home to the 1.58-mile running track that surrounds it, where thousands of New Yorkers exercise every day.

CHARLOTTE & HARRY'S APARTMENT
PARK AVENUE AT 81ST STREET

This Italian Renaissance palazzo-style apartment building is located in the city's posh Carnegie Hill neighborhood. The building was only used for exterior shots in the movie; the interior scenes were all shot on a soundstage.

CHRISTIE'S
49TH STREET BETWEEN
5TH & 6TH AVENUES

Where the girls attend Blair Elkenn's jewelry auction

Founded in 1776, Christie's is one of the world's leading auction houses. The house conducts more than six hundred sales annually in categories including fine and decorative arts, photography, collectibles, automobiles, wine, and jewelry.

THE COFFEE SHOP
GREENE STREET

Where the girls have brunch and talk sex

There is not an actual coffee shop at this location, but—in an effort to re-create the signature coffee shop from the series—the crew built one in an empty store in the city's trendy SoHo neighborhood.

THE CONDÉ NAST BUILDING
42ND STREET
BETWEEN BROADWAY & 6TH AVENUE

Where Carrie meets with Enid at Vogue

This building houses the Condé Nast empire, which includes magazines such as *The New Yorker*, *Vanity Fair*, *Lucky*, *Glamour*—and, of course, *Vogue*. Completed in June 1999 by the Durst Organization, the sleek, modern tower was the first new office in the newly redeveloped Times Square.

DIANE VON FURSTENBERG
WASHINGTON STREET
BETWEEN 13TH & 14TH STREETS

Where Carrie calls Samantha to tell her she and Big are getting engaged and the girls celebrate Samantha's fiftieth birthday (interior)

The DVF flagship store opened in the spring of 2007, offering Furstenberg's trademark wrap dresses as well as shoes and other items. While obviously not a club, the crew decided to turn the upstairs workroom into one for the final scene of the movie after falling in love with the openness of space.

DUANE READE
BROADWAY & 18TH STREET

Where Miranda shops for a Halloween costume with Carrie

The first Duane Reade drugstore opened in 1960 on Broadway between Duane and Reade streets in Tribeca. Today, the chain is a New York institution, with more than 230 stores in operation throughout the New York metropolitan area.

GOOD WORLD BAR & GRILL
ORCHARD STREET AT DIVISION STREET

Where Miranda and family have dinner together

Although it stands in for a Brooklyn Italian restaurant in the film, Good World is actually a hip bar and restaurant located in Chinatown, specializing in Swedish appetizers. The crew added checkered tablecloths and fancy bottles with melted wax on them to make the place look authentically Italian.

HOTEL GIRAFFE
PARK AVENUE SOUTH AT 26TH STREET

Big's sublet

This posh boutique hotel, located in the Flatiron District, opened in December 1999. The crew used the hotel's twenty-third-floor events room for Big's sublet, taking advantage of its stunning views of the Manhattan cityscape.

LA FOCACCIA
BANK STREET AT WEST 4TH STREET

Where Carrie meets Louise and her boyfriend

This casual Greenwich Village pizza place offers a cozy atmosphere, complete with a wood-burning fireplace and large windows perfect for people-watching.

LUCE PLAN
GREENE STREET
BETWEEN BROOME & GRAND STREETS

Where Carrie goes shopping for a new desk with Charlotte

This Italian lighting shop, which opened in the spring of 2007, was converted into an upscale furniture store for the film.

LUMI
LEXINGTON AVENUE AT 70TH STREET

Where Charlotte runs into Big at lunch

This Tuscan restaurant has been an Upper East Side fixture since 1995. Its tranquil dining room features a fireplace and cozy banquettes.

THE MERCER HOTEL AND MERCER KITCHEN
MERCER STREET AT PRINCE STREET

Miranda's temporary home after she leaves Steve

This luxury SoHo hotel is known for its modern design and its appeal to visiting celebrities. The Mercer Kitchen serves American Provençal cuisine by world renowned chef and restauranteur Jean-Georges Vongerichten.

MIRANDA'S POST-BREAKUP APARTMENT
HENRY STREET
BETWEEN RUTGERS & JEFFERSON STREETS

This building is located in a transitional neighborhood between the Lower East Side and Chinatown, known for its cultural diversity.

THE MODERN
53RD STREET
BETWEEN 5TH & 6TH AVENUES

Where Carrie tells Charlotte and Miranda she and Big are getting married

This upscale restaurant and bar at the Museum of Modern Art offers tranquil views of the museum's Aldrich Rockefeller Sculpture Garden.

THE NEW YORK PUBLIC LIBRARY
FIFTH AVENUE
BETWEEN 40TH & 42ND STREETS

Where Big jilts Carrie on their wedding day

A stately Beaux-Arts building houses the main branch of the New York Public Library, which opened in 1911. Its entrance is flanked by two iconic stone lions, nicknamed Patience and Fortitude. The Library may indeed be rented for private events such as weddings, which can be held in any of three breathtaking spaces: Astor Hall, the Celeste Bartos Forum, or the McGraw Rotunda.

RAOUL'S
PRINCE STREET
BETWEEN THOMPSON & SULLIVAN STREETS

Where Carrie and Miranda have Valentine's Day dinner

SoHo's original French bistro, Raoul's packs in the crowds night after night with its no-frills menu—written entirely on chalkboards—and friendly neighborhood atmosphere.

STARBUCKS
ASTOR PLACE
BETWEEN BROADWAY AND LAFAYETTE ST.

Where Carrie interviews Louise

This East Village coffee shop is one of Manhattan's most frequented Starbucks, located right next to the bustling Astor Place subway station. It is popular with local college students as well as freelancers, who are known to use it as an impromptu office space.

VITRA
NINTH AVENUE
BETWEEN 13TH & 14TH STREETS

Where the girls celebrate Samantha's fiftieth birthday (exterior)

The sleek, transparent facade of this modern furniture seller in the Meatpacking District made the perfect backdrop for the film's final scene.

BROOKLYN

THE BROOKLYN BRIDGE

Where Miranda and Steve reconcile

Built in 1883, this iconic bridge connects Brooklyn to Manhattan, and as such, marked the birth of New York City as we know it. An attraction for cyclists, walkers, and tourists from all over the world, it features stunning views of the Brooklyn and Manhattan skylines and is the perfect location for a romantic reconciliation.

BROOKLYN SUPREME COURT
ADAMS STREET BETWEEN
JORALEMON & JOHNSON STREETS

Where Big and Carrie marry

Many a Brooklynite has endured jury duty at this courthouse, which doubles as Manhattan's City Hall in the film. The crew ended up only shooting inside, so as to keep the ending a surprise.

JUNIOR'S
FLATBUSH AVENUE AT DEKALB AVENUE

Where Carrie, Big, and friends eat brunch after the wedding

Founded by Harry Rosen in 1950, Junior's is a Brooklyn institution, known

the world over for its stupendous cheesecake. Located in a newly revitalized section of downtown Brooklyn, the restaurant has become a haven for a new generation of Brooklynites, who are known to stop in for a bite to eat after a long night of clubbing.

MIRANDA AND STEVE'S HOUSE
DEKALB AVENUE BETWEEN
WASHINGTON & WAVERLY AVENUES

This Brooklyn brownstone is the same house that was used for Miranda and Steve's house during the series—and it is still owned by the same family. Because the house was somewhat unfinished inside, the crew did some trim and plaster work and refinished the wood staircase.

LOS ANGELES

GUCCI
NORTH RODEO DRIVE BETWEEN
DAYTON & BRIGHTON WAYS

Where Samantha goes shopping with her dog

This outpost of the iconic Italian fashion label is located in L.A.'s posh Beverly Hills neighborhood.

SAMANTHA AND SMITH'S BEACH HOUSE
MALIBU ROAD

This ultramodern house is quintessential L.A., with three stories of balconies and terraces and floor-to-ceiling windows that offer spectacular views of the ocean.

Special Thanks
Melinda Relyea
Sarah Jessica Parker
Eric Cyphers
Michael Patrick King
and everyone at *Sex and the City* and New Line who
has participated in and given their time for this book

Thanks
Bronwyn Barnes, Mark Beckelman, Craig Blankenhorn, Edward Bolkus,
William Bostwick, David E. Brown, Kim Cattrall, Joe Collins, Sarah
Condon, Bree Conover, Jeremy Conway, James Costos, Francis Coy,
Kristin Davis, Daniel del Valle, Max Dickstein, David Eigenberg, Jeff Elkins,
Alissa Faden, Patricia Field, Willie Garson, Evan Handler, Andrea Henry,
Mei Lai Hippisley-Coxe, Riley Hooker, Jennifer Hudson, David Imhoff, Coco
Joly, Gurmeet Kaur, JaEl Labriel, Lydia Marks, Shelby Meizlick, John Melfi,
Lauren Nathan, Ingrid L. C. Nilsen, Cynthia Nixon, Emily Oberman, Mary
Ellen O'Neill, Tiffany D. H. Parker, Richard Petrucci, Anna Rabinovitch,
Amy Rivera, Molly Rogers, Steve Ross, Holly Rothman, Jeff Scher, Margot
Schupf, Rebecca Sides, Bonnie Siegler, Lindsey Stanberry, Emma Tait,
Alex Tart, Ina Treciokas, Anna Wahrman, Betty Wong, and Jessica Zadnik

Photo Credits
All photographs by Craig Blankenhorn/© MMVIII
New Line Productions, Inc., except for the following:
Page 10: (bottom right) courtesy of Mei Lai Hippisley-Coxe; page 11: script and
storyboards courtesy of Michael Patrick King, (bottom) courtesy of Melinda
Relyea; page 12: (top left and bottom right inset) courtesy of Melinda Relyea;
pages 12–13: (top center) courtesy of Mei Lai Hippisley-Coxe; page 13: (top
right) courtesy of Mei Lai Hippisley-Coxe; page 14: (top right) courtesy of Mei
Lai Hippisley-Coxe; pages 16–23: Craig Blankenhorn/HBO; page 40: (top
left) *New York Post* logo reprinted courtesy of the *New York Post*, (left) Craig
Blankenhorn/HBO; page 43: (top left) courtesy of Melinda Relyea; page 50:
Vivienne Westwood note courtesy of the *Sex and the City* prop department;
page 54: (top) © Peter Aaron/Esto; page 57: coloring book courtesy of the
Sex and the City prop department; page 60: (background image of Central
Park) Panoramic Images/Getty Images; page 85: courtesy of Melinda
Relyea; page 88: inset photo courtesy of Daniel del Valle; pages 106–107:
(bottom) Craig Blankenhorn/HBO; page 110: courtesy of the *Sex and the
City* prop department; page 111: "Love" keychain courtesy of the *Sex and the
City* prop department; page 155: (photos) Craig Blankenhorn/HBO, book covers
courtesy of the *Sex and the City* art department; page 162: (top row, second from
left) courtesy of Mei Lai Hippisley-Coxe, (bottom row, first from left) courtesy of
Mei Lai Hippisley-Coxe; page 163: (bottom row, second from right) courtesy of
Mei Lai Hippisley-Coxe; page 164: (top row, second from left) courtesy of Mei Lai
Hippisley-Coxe; page 165: (middle row, second and third from right) courtesy of
Mei Lai Hippisley-Coxe; pages 173–175: All photos courtesy of Jeff Scher except
for the following: 173: (top row, third from left) Harvey Silikovitz/© iStockphoto.
com, (second row, first from left) PictureArts/Newscom, (third row, first from left)
courtesy of the *Sex and the City* locations department, (third row, second from left)
age fotostock/Superstock, (third row, third from left) courtesy of the *Sex and the
City* prop department; page 174: (top row, first from left) courtesy of the *Sex and the
City* locations department, (bottom row) courtesy of the *Sex and the City* locations
department; page 175: (top row, first from left) courtesy of the *Sex and the City*
locations department, (second row, third from left) courtesy of the *Sex and the City*
locations department.

This book was produced by

 **MELCHER
MEDIA**

124 West 13th Street
New York, NY 10011
www.melcher.com

PUBLISHER: Charles Melcher
ASSOCIATE PUBLISHER: Bonnie Eldon
EDITOR IN CHIEF: Duncan Bock

EXECUTIVE EDITOR: Lia Ronnen
PROJECT EDITORS: Jessi Rymill & Megan Worman
ASSOCIATE EDITOR: Shoshana Thaler
PRODUCTION DIRECTOR: Kurt Andrews

DESIGN: Number Seventeen, New York